In Praise of Roy Peter Clark's
HOW TO WRITE SHORT

"A fun, practical guide to writing little from a guy who's written a lot. Respected journalist and writing teacher Roy Peter Clark really knows his way around a sentence. Learn from him." —Christopher Johnson, author of *Microstyle*

"*How to Write Short* comes at the perfect time and enshrines Roy Peter Clark as America's best writing coach. Who else could masterfully tease the secrets of short, powerful writing from unexpected sources—the Bible, Shakespeare, Tom Petty, and Abe Lincoln? This book should be on every serious writer's shelf... underpants."

—Ben Montgomery, staff writer, *Tampa Bay Times*
(If you are wondering about that last word,
it's an inside joke from the book!)

"We're writing more than ever before, on screens big and small, and the pressure is on to make our characters count. In this book, Roy Peter Clark shows us how, and more importantly, why it's worth the effort. *How to Write Short* is both a deeply practical guidebook and an annotated collection of concise gems from some of the world's greatest writers and journalists, not one of them longer than 300 words. Roy's message is clear: great writing is a matter of craft, not word count. *How to Write Short* will make you a better writer at any length."

—Robin Sloan, author of *Mr. Penumbra's
24-Hour Bookstore*

"Roy Peter Clark has compressed a lifetime of learning and love of language into *How to Write Short*. An engaging, entertaining, indispensable guide to the art and craft of concision."
— James Geary, author of *The World in a Phrase* and *I Is an Other*

"*How to Write Short* both instructs and delights, in equal measure. On every page there is some useful advice and an amusing observation or illustration. Roy Peter Clark's many fans know that (extremely) diverse examples are one of his specialties, and this book doesn't disappoint. Open it up at random and you'll find quotes from Oscar Wilde, Steven Wright, Dorothy Parker, and Gypsy Rose Lee. And that's just one page! Read this book!"
— Ben Yagoda, author of *When You Catch an Adjective, Kill It* and *How to Not Write Bad*

HOW
TO WRITE
SHORT

ALSO BY ROY PETER CLARK

Writing Tools
The Glamour of Grammar
Help! For Writers

HOW TO WRITE SHORT

WORD CRAFT FOR
FAST TIMES

by

ROY PETER CLARK

LITTLE, BROWN AND COMPANY
NEW YORK   BOSTON   LONDON

To Gene Patterson

"Don't just make a living, make a mark."

~~~

Little, Brown and Company
Hachette Book Group
237 Park Avenue, New York, NY 10017
littlebrown.com

First Edition: August 2013

Little, Brown and Company is a division of Hachette Book Group, Inc. The Little, Brown name and logo are trademarks of Hachette Book Group, Inc.

The publisher is not responsible for websites (or their content) that are not owned by the publisher.

The Hachette Speakers Bureau provides a wide range of authors for speaking events. To find out more, go to hachettespeakersbureau.com or call (866) 376-6591.

Copyright acknowledgments appear on pages 241–247.

Library of Congress Cataloging-in-Publication Data
Clark, Roy Peter.
   How to write short: word craft for fast times / by Roy Peter Clark.—First Edition.
      p. cm.
   Includes index.
   ISBN 978-0-316-20435-4
   1. English language—Rhetoric.   2. Report writing.   I. Title.
   PE1408.C4175 2013
   808'.042—dc23   2012039692

10 9 8 7 6 5 4 3 2

RRD-C

Printed in the United States of America

CONTENTS

CONTENTS

HOW
TO WRITE
SHORT

When Words Are Worth a Thousand Pictures

At this moment, the right pocket in my jeans contains more computing power than the space vessel that carried the first astronauts to the moon. My Apple iPhone 4S stores all of Shakespeare's plays, a searchable source I can use for quick reference. More often, I use my mobile phone for access to what are no longer being called "new" forms of information delivery: blog posts, e-mails, text messages, YouTube videos, 140-character tweets, and Facebook updates, not to mention games, weather reports, Google Maps, coupons, the White House, Al Jazeera, NPR, dozens of newspapers, music sites, an electronic drum set, an app that imitates the sounds of *Star Wars* lightsabers, one that turns your photo into an image of a zombie, and yet another invaluable resource titled Atomic Fart, which turns your mobile device into an electronic whoopee cushion.

Toto, we are not in Kansas anymore. In fact, we're soaring high above Oz, looking down like a Google Earth search. We're high on technology, but adrift in a jet stream of information. All the more reason to write short — and well.

I've written *How to Write Short* because I could not find another book quite like it and because in the digital age, short writing is king. We need more good short writing — the kind that makes us stop, read, and think — in an accelerating world. A time-starved culture bloated with information hungers for the lean, clean, simple, and direct. Such is our appetite for short writing that not only do our *long* stories seem too long, but our *short* stories feel too long as well.

The most important messages are short, after all: "Amen, brother." "Will you marry me?" "I do." "Not guilty." "The Giants win the pennant!" (That message was so exciting in 1951 that the radio announcer Russ Hodges repeated it five times.) "Score!" "You're fired." "I love you."

In his book *Microstyle: The Art of Writing Little,* Christopher Johnson writes, "Messages of just a word, a phrase, or a short sentence or two — *micromessages* — lean heavily on every word and live or die by the tiniest stylistic choices. Micromessages depend not on the elements of style but on the *atoms* of style." To which I would add, "Not just the atoms of style but the quirks and quarks of style as well."

The *New York Times* reported the death of Osama Bin Laden with a two-tier headline of fifteen words. On the other hand, the *St. Petersburg Times* chose a single word for its headline—DEAD—but printed it in letters that were five inches high.

More than four hundred years ago, William Shakespeare built his fame on the construction of thirty-seven plays, more or less, at least half of them masterpieces. But he also penned 154 love poems called sonnets, each exactly fourteen lines in length. The Bard demonstrated how long and short writing can coexist. For the first fourteen lines of *Romeo and Juliet,* he composed a sonnet that summarizes the key plot elements, including (spoiler alert!) the news that "a pair of star-cross'd lovers take their life."

To cut down the number of words we moderns use, we could revert to Sumerian cuneiform on clay tablets or Egyptian hieroglyphics on papyrus scrolls. They say, after all, that a picture is worth a thousand words. I have seen some pictures that were worth a thousand words, but being a man of the word, I remain open to the idea that some words may be worth a thousand pictures. Consider these historical and cultural documents:

The Hippocratic oath
The Twenty-Third Psalm
The Lord's Prayer
Shakespeare's Sonnet 18
The Preamble to the Constitution
The Gettysburg Address
The last paragraph of Dr. King's "I Have a Dream" speech

I once exchanged messages with NPR's Scott Simon, who shared this important idea, which he learned from his stepfather: If you add up the words in these documents, the sum will be fewer than a thousand, 996 by my count. Show me any number of pictures as powerful as those seven documents.

Now meet Joanna Smith, a young reporter for the *Toronto Star*. Picture her, early in 2010, hitting the ground in Haiti, a country rocked by earthquake. She will file dispatches by the minute using Twitter. Smith posts dozens of short reports in the form of tweets, each limited to 140 characters: "Fugitive from prison caught looting, taken from police, beaten, dragged thru street, died slowly and set on fire in pile of garbage." One by one, each post is a vivid snapshot of natural and human disaster. Together they constitute something akin to a serial narrative with short chapters, or a "live blog."

Writers who complain about a 140-character limit are, shall we say, shortsighted. But consider this array of sentences, expressed easily within the tight boundaries of a tweet:

- "These are the times that try men's souls."
- "The reports of my death are greatly exaggerated."
- "Take my wife, please."
- "Where's the beef?"
- "I like Ike."

That list includes a famous line from a political pamphlet by Thomas Paine, a telegram from Mark Twain, a joke by Henny Youngman, an advertising campaign for Wendy's, and a presidential political slogan. When I add them up, I get 138 characters. One tweet.

So the culture turns: short, shorter, even shorter, abbreviation, acronym, emoticon. Maybe explorers from a future generation will discover that our discourse devolved to the point that combinations of smiley and frowny faces could be used as the binary elements to express everything from love poems to eulogies to State of the Union addresses.

Now for the good news: writing in short forms does not require the sacrifice of literary values. The poet Peter Meinke talks about the power that comes from focus, wit, and polish. *Focus* is the unifying theme. *Wit* is the governing intelligence. *Polish* creates the sparkle that comes from careful word choice and revision.

The demand for good short writing is not an innovation. That need can be traced, through countless examples, back to the origins of writing itself. Here, for example, is a list, not exhaustive, of forms of short writing that users of the Internet have inherited in one way or another: prayers, epigrams, wisdom literature, epitaphs, short poetic forms (such as haiku, sonnet, couplet), language on monuments, letters, rules of thumb, labels (as on poison bottles), lyrics, ship logs, diaries, journal entries, bumper stickers, graffiti, advertisements, news dispatches, pieces of dialogue or conversation, wedding and other announcements, headlines, captions, summaries, telegrams, notes, microfiction, insults—and the list goes on.

From the analysis of these traditional short forms, writers and readers can learn the essential elements of good short writing, everything from word order, ellipses, and slang to levels of formality and informality, details, and parallel structures. These same strategies and more can be used to great effect in the new forms that have emerged with the development of digital technology: e-mail, instant messaging, text messages, blog posts, hyperlinks, website writing and navigation, commentary, feedback loops, updates, headlines, summaries, search engine optimization (phrases that will get you high up on Google searches), Q & A's, slide shows.

My study of short writing over the centuries reveals that while technologies, genres, and platforms evolve, the purposes of short writing remain intact:

- To enshrine: gravestones, monuments, tattoos
- To amuse: jokes, insults, one-liners, snarky comments
- To explain: museum texts, recipes, instructions
- To narrate: microfiction, live blogs, diaries
- To alert and inform: text messages, tweets, telegrams, status updates, news bulletins, signage
- To remember: notes, summaries, lists, ceremonial texts (such as wedding vows)
- To inspire: proverbs, quotations, prayers, aphorisms
- To sell: graffiti, adverts, résumés, bumper stickers, T-shirts, dating sites
- To converse: Q & A, social networks, feedback loops, blogs, speech balloons

You can detect from these partial lists that the craft of short writing applies to all forms of expression, not just the techie ones. Most writers will be as concerned with practical, job-related forms of short writing—from letters of recommendation and complaint to job postings, pitch notes, product descriptions, and classified ads—as they are with postings on social networks.

How short is short? Common sense dictates that length is relative. I am about five feet eleven inches tall, a little above average for American men. That means that I am too large to ride a horse in the Kentucky Derby and too small to play defensive tackle for the Tampa Bay Buccaneers.

A short story can be more than three thousand words long, which might be the length of a substantial essay or the longest story in Sunday's *New York Times*. A three-hundred-word piece of writing is short by most standards, but not if you are writing a tweet. Still, for the purposes of this book, three hundred words seems a reasonable boundary for learning how to read, write, and talk about short writing.

I've divided this book into two sections, the *how* and the *why* of the short writing craft. The *how* comprises the rhetorical strategies that make a short text tick. The *why* reveals the practical uses of short writing over centuries, the ways in which writers use short forms to fulfill their aspirations, from the quotidian to the eternal.

This introduction turns out to be about sixteen hundred words, twice the length needed to print the Ten Commandments, the Hail Mary, the first stanza of Dante's *Divine Comedy*, the Emma Lazarus poem on the pedestal of the Statue of Liberty, the lyrics to "Over the Rainbow," and the words recited by Neil Armstrong when he stepped onto the surface of the moon. I guess I've got a little more work to do to master the exquisite craft of how to write short — especially in these fast times.

I

~~~

How to Write Short

The problem of writing short is exemplified by this anecdote, published in the *New York Times*, about the famed novelist E. L. Doctorow:

> One morning at breakfast, when she was in the first or second grade, E. L. Doctorow's daughter, Caroline, asked her father to write a note explaining her absence from school, due to a cold, the previous day. Doctorow began, "My daughter, Caroline...." He stopped. "Of course she's my daughter," he said to himself. "Who else would be writing a note for her?" He began again. "Please excuse Caroline Doctorow...." He stopped again. "Why do I have to beg and plead for her?" he said. "She had a virus.

She didn't commit a crime!" On he went, note after failed note, until a pile of crumpled pages lay at his feet. Finally, his wife, Helen, said, "I can't take this anymore," penned a perfect note and sent Caroline off to school. Doctorow concluded: "Writing is very difficult, especially in the short form."

When it comes to the how of short writing, you will find three paths: learning short writing through reading; practicing the best short writing moves; and cutting longer texts down to size. If you want to write short, you must read short, and you must do it without bias. Yes, your reading will include classic poems and other gems of human culture, but the clever writer can never discriminate against the funkier or more utilitarian examples of the craft. The baseball card, the limerick, the lyric, the ransom note, the fortune in the fortune cookie — each stands as a work with a sharp rhetorical purpose and a clearly imagined audience.

Close reading of short forms reveals the most strategic moves practiced by the best writers. To grow in the craft, we study those moves, name them, imitate them, and adapt them till they conform to our own sense of mission and begin to sound like us.

A hard part of the writing process is cutting, and yes, Mr. Doctorow, the pain is magnified when the writing is short. Comparing it to surgery on the human body, cutting our prose moves us from excess fat to basic fat to muscle to bone to marrow and even deeper. During revision, I realize that 90 percent of my cuts are helpful. I want to keep cutting the clutter, but I reach a point where it's hard to know what to cut and what to keep. The final cuts are hardest because they can identify nuances of meaning (think of the sculptor's final touches) or they can threaten something essential to the reader's understanding. An editor or test reader can come to the writer's rescue. It is often those final cuts — the finishing touches — that create the most dazzling facets of the diamond, a jewel of short writing, ready to be polished. How and when do we make those crucial cuts?

When we have worked our way through the how of short writing, we will be ready to tackle the why.

1

Collect short writing.

Remember the movie kid who said, "I see dead people"?

I see short writing.

I collect it all in my daybook: haikus and sonnets, aphorisms and parables, prayers and insults, bumper sticker slogans and T-shirt rhymes, blurbs, titles, ads, street signs, marginalia, bulleted lists, song lyrics, announcements, propaganda, and names, names, and more names. I can also go new-school: tweets, blog posts, updates on social networks, e-mails, text messages, and more.

I'm in an airport motel in Providence, Rhode Island, toweling off after a shower, when my eye catches a green tag hooked onto the towel rack.

"Reuse or replace?" it reads.

And then: "To reuse: hang towels up; to replace: place towels on floor."

Then at the bottom: "Take care. We owe it to one another."

The style is spare. Absent are words such as *environment, sustainability,* or *climate change.* The messenger counts on my knowing the backstory: that needless laundering of towels helps no one. The slight message does heavy work. It offers readers a choice, then a course of action and, as in a parable, a moral as a reward.

I prowl the stacks at a bookstore near Brown University called Books on the Square. A volume called *The Notebook* catches my eye. The author is José Saramago of Portugal, a winner of the Nobel Prize in Literature. In short daily passages from September 2008 to November 2009 the author chronicles the final year of his life, offering sharp opinions on politics, literature, and culture. Some entries measure five hundred words or more, but the average length is shorter. Before it became a book, the entries ran as blog posts.

It fills me with joy that an eighty-seven-year-old author would keep a blog. He stands with the octogenarian golf writer Dan Jenkins, who still reports on tournaments live via Twitter. A third musketeer could be Herman Wouk, who is publishing—at the age of ninety-seven—an epistolary novel narrated through not just letters but e-mails, text messages, and tweets.

Saramago blogs on November 25, 2008, after a press conference in São Paulo, Brazil:

> I was surprised that several journalists wanted to ask me about my role as a blogger...my decision to write on the "infinite page of the Internet." Could it be, to put it more

clearly, that it's here that we all most closely resemble one another? Is this the closest thing we have to citizen power? Are we more companionable when we write on the Internet? I have no answers; I'm merely stating the questions. And I enjoy writing here now. I don't know whether it is more democratic, I only know that I feel just the same as the young man with the wild hair and the round-rimmed glasses, in his early twenties, who was asking me...questions. For a blog, no doubt.

This passage ends with a delightful jolt, a standard move in clever short writing. That intentional sentence fragment stops the paragraph short, a passage that rolls downhill from a first-person statement to a meditation on writing, technology, and democracy to a vivid physical description of a young blogger — all hitting a full stop with the starkest language, five one-syllable words needing just fifteen letters.

But Saramago can go shorter. Consider his take on the economic/political summit known as G20:

On the subject of the chimera that is the G20, just three questions:
Why?
What for?
For whom?

Here the text reveals the effect of a single elegant word — a grace note — in an otherwise straightforward composition. That word is *chimera*. It means "illusion," or what the dictionary defines as "a fabrication of the mind." But that meaning has been abstracted from the original. In Greek mythology, the chimera was an imaginary hybrid creature: "a fire-breathing she-monster ... having a lion's head, a goat's body, and a serpent's tail." That metaphor transforms twenty "heads" of state into a power-hungry monster with twenty heads.

What shall we say about the nature of short writing for those, such as Saramago, who are best known for writing long? Is the short piece a distillation of something much more substantial?

In a preface to *The Notebook,* the Italian novelist Umberto Eco offers this reflection:

> I am writing this preface because I feel I have an experience in common with our friend Saramago, and this is of writing books on the one hand, and on the other of writing moral critiques in a weekly magazine. Since the second type of writing is clearer and more popular than the former, lots of people have asked me if I haven't decanted into the little articles wider reflections from the bigger books. But no, I reply, experience teaches me ... that it is the impulse of irritation, the satirical sting, the ruthless criticism written on the spur of the moment that will go on to supply material for an essayistic reflection or a more extended narrative. It is everyday writing that inspires the most committed works, not the other way round.

In other words, if you want to write long, begin by writing short.

If your goal is to write short and well, you must begin by reading the best short writing you can find. Start by keeping a "commonplace book," a notebook that contains treasured short passages from favorite authors next to bits and pieces of your own writing.

A great collector of short, vivid language was Dale Carnegie, who inspired millions of readers with his midwestern common sense and pragmatic optimism. His own phrases were quoted countless times, perhaps because he spent formative years storing the wisdom of others.

In an introduction to an anthology titled *Dale Carnegie's Scrapbook,* Dorothy Carnegie explains, "Dale Carnegie was a man who loved the tang of a salty phrase. In all of his reading, the hooks of his attention were barbed to catch the pungent paragraph, the apt expression, the sweeping sentence that thereafter remained fixed in his memory."

On random pages the scrapbook stores quotes from Helen Keller, Winston Churchill, Emily Dickinson, and Theodore Roosevelt, along with Washington, Franklin, Emerson, and many more. Gertrude Stein ("I like familiarity. In me it does not breed contempt. Only more familiarity") bumps into Wilbur Wright ("A parrot talks much but flies little").

In his book *The Man Who Made Lists,* Joshua Kendall describes the life of Peter Roget, who gave us the world-famous thesaurus. As a young boy, Roget kept notebooks in which he listed words that described all aspects of his little world. "At the heart of Peter's childhood notebook are his word lists," writes Kendall, "written in a neat hand and consisting of Latin words juxtaposed with their English meanings, grouped under categories such as 'Beasts,' 'People,' 'Parts of the Body,' 'Of Writing, Reading, etc.,' 'In the Garden,' 'Of the Weather,'" and many more.

Roget would have been a fan of Ben Schott's *Original Miscellany,* a tiny volume filled with both practical knowledge and interesting curiosities. The Twelve Labors of Hercules rub up against the names of Santa's reindeer; World War II postal acronyms (BURMA: be upstairs ready, my angel) from soldiers to their sweethearts back home sit nicely upon a list of Internet emoticons including "wearing a turban": @:-). Quotations from Samuel Johnson abound, including this one on the last page:

> There is nothing, Sir, too little for so little a creature as man. It is by studying little things that we attain the great art of having as little misery and as much happiness as possible.

Let it be, Dr. Johnson, let it be.

GRACE NOTES

1. Keep a daybook devoted to short writing.

2. Include examples of great short writing collected from other sources.

3. Write short pieces of your own inspired by the ones you've collected.

4. Over time, examine your short writing for seeds of longer pieces.

5. Practice writing plain sentences that contain a grace note, one interesting word that stands out, such as Saramago's *chimera*.

6. You will run into great short writing in the most surprising places, from restaurant menus to rest room walls. Record these in your daybook or snap a photo with your cell phone.

2

Study short writing wherever it finds you.

When it comes to the English language, writers cannot afford to be snobs. I may study the language of a writer such as Robert Louis Stevenson, the author of *Kidnapped*, but I am even more interested in the mangled language of a real ransom note.

> Dear Sir!
> Have 50.000$ redy 25.000$ in
> 20$ bills 15.000$ in 10$ bills and
> 10.000$ in 5$ bills After 2–4 days
> we will inform you were to deliver
> the mony.
>
> We warn you for making
> anyding public or for notify the Police

The child is in gut care.
Indication for all letters are
singnature

and three hohls.

This note, one of several delivered after the kidnapping of the Lindbergh baby in 1932, became a key piece of evidence in the conviction and execution of Bruno Hauptmann for the crime. The grammatical mistakes and phonetic spelling were the first clues that the kidnapper was of German descent.

The British author David Lodge says it best: a novelist, or any writer, "cannot afford to cut himself off from low, vulgar, debased language." Nothing expressed in language is irrelevant for the learning writer, not the chants of soccer hooligans or the list of ingredients on a box of cake mix.

My reading and writing career, for example, began with baseball cards.

I was a first grader when I learned to decode the letters on the pages of my Dick and Jane reading primers, and while the "stories" in those books were stultifying, there was a genuine thrill of discovery in turning those letters into sounds and those sounds into meaning.

But because I was born in New York City in 1948, my little existence was electrified by the golden age of baseball. I owned boxes and boxes of baseball cards, which we collected, traded, and "flipped" in a variety of competitive games. The cards—which back then came with slabs of fragrant bubble gum—featured images of the players, sometimes in photographic portraits, sometimes in action. I still own a few favorite cards, including five from the career of the famed baseball man Don Zimmer, who has now spent more than sixty years in baseball as a player, coach, manager, and consultant.

His 1954 card describes him as a prospect for the Brooklyn Dodgers: "Don was leading the American Association in Home Runs and Runs Batted In, July 7, 1953, when he was struck in the head by a pitch, missing the remainder of the season.... Don has aspirations to some day become a Major League manager [irony unintended!]" A cartoon at the bottom of the card shows a bride and groom surrounded by baseball players: "He and Miss Jean Bauerle were married at home plate in Elmira, N.Y., August 18, 1951."

It was from these brief texts in small print on the backs of pieces of cardboard that I learned not just the background of the players but the rules of the game, its history and traditions, and, best of all, its language and slang: A "blue dart" was a line drive. A "can of corn" was an easy pop fly. "Chin music" was a pitch up and in.

It took me years and years to get out of the habit of reading the backs of cereal boxes as I ate my Wheaties or Rice Krispies. There was adventure in those texts back then, promises of special prizes inside the box, trinkets such as siren whistles and magnifying glasses, or stories about famous athletes like Lou Gehrig.

The boxes are not as interesting these days, but I have saved a beauty, a box of Kellogg's Raisin Bran from 2003. The phrase "Two Scoops!" is prominent on the front. On one side panel, under the phrase "High In Fiber," is a list of nutrition facts. But the jackpot for breakfast table readers is on the back, a quiz that asks you to match up short quotations with the famous people who uttered them.

Who said, "If my husband ever met a woman on the street who looked like the women in his paintings, he would faint"? OK, that has to be Mrs. Pablo Picasso. Correct. (Answers are on the inside of the box.) "Be nice to people on your way up because you might meet 'em on your way down"? Sounds like the gritty New York City talk of Jimmy Durante. Correct! (OK, so I got 16 out of 18 wrong.)

Short writing experiments assault me from every direction. I find six hundred websites devoted to fortune cookie messages, including the following:

- "Bread today is better than cake tomorrow."
- "A feeling is an idea with roots."
- "Cookie says 'You crack me up.'"

And my favorite: "Ignore previous cookie."

There may not be a smaller tablet space for short writing than those heart-shaped Valentine candies carrying love messages. My favorites are the old-school "Oh you kid" and "Hubba hubba," with these new ones for journalists, submitted by an author named j-love:

- "Luv byte"
- "I'm ur tease"
- "Hot scoop"
- "Im-press me"

- "Lede me on"
- "Sexy syntax"
- "Pxl8 me"

Look at the sources of short writing gathered for this chapter, from ransom notes to baseball cards to cookie fortunes to heart candies.

Short texts written for one reason can be creatively repurposed for just the right occasion. Consider my encounter with an old-fashioned nautical ship's wheel, used as a decoration at the Bayboro Cafe in St. Petersburg. As I read the settings for steering, I noticed that the progression of words could stand for romantic progress, a voyage on the sea of love:

Let Go
   Slack Away
      All Clear
         Ahead Slow
            Stop
            Astern Slow
         Not Clear
      Heave In
   Make Fast
Docking

Prepare yourself to find interesting short texts in strange and surprising places. Some clever authors, especially in the postmodern era, look for unusual spaces to fill with text. No writer is better known for this than Dave Eggers, especially in the appendices to the paperback edition of his book *A Heartbreaking Work of Staggering Genius*. Among the least literary spaces in a book is the copyright page, so what is the reader to make of this from Eggers?

> The author wishes to reserve the right to use spaces like this, and to work within them, for no other reason than it entertains him and a small coterie of readers. It does not mean that anything ironic is happening. It does not mean that someone is being *pomo* or *meta* or *cute*. It simply means that someone is writing in small type, in a space usually devoted to the copyright information, because doing so is fun. It has no far-reaching implications for the art, nor does it say anything of importance about the author, or his contemporaries, or his predecessors, or successors. It is simply the use of a space because that space is there, and the use of it is entertaining. It should not make you angry, and it should not influence in any important way your reading of this appendix, or the book it appendicizes.

Write short in surprising spaces.

An epilogue: Just a few days ago I ran into Beau Zimmer, a young Florida journalist and a grandson of Don Zimmer. "Please extend to your grandparents my warmest wishes on their sixtieth wedding anniversary," I said. "I know they were married at home plate in Elmira, New York."

"You must have owned his baseball card," said Beau.

GRACE NOTES

1. Imagine that an anti–Valentine's Day movement swept America. You would still give out little heart candies, but the messages would now reflect disgust, disappointment, disillusion. Write ten that are better than "Eat your heart out."

2. Make believe that fortune cookies were served at all ethnic restaurants. How would the fortunes read at, say, a New York–style Italian restaurant? "Fuhgeddaboudit!" or "Stop reading, you meatball, and EAT!" Try this with a variety of ethnicities.

3. By definition, your early language experiences involved short texts such as nursery rhymes or song lyrics for kids. For me, it was "Ring-around-the-rosy," with its secret associations with the plague. Find one of your buried treasures, research its origins, and write about it in your daybook.

4. Write a brief premise for a movie in which something discovered in a pack of baseball cards proves crucial.

5. Write a summary of a fictional story in which a message in a bottle proves to be pivotal.

3

~~~

Read for focus.

Even when we read long works, we can still read for focus. While the big parts need a focus, so do the smaller parts: sections, chapters, vignettes, anecdotes, paragraphs. Frank Deford, one of America's most popular and versatile writers, knows about focus. In this paragraph he homes in on the practical economics in the year 1898, as exemplified by the Uneeda company's charging five cents for a package of crackers:

> Uneeda knew pricing. The nickel was king in America at this time. It was so common a currency that the dime was, often as not, called a "double nickel." You didn't want to get stuck with a wooden nickel. The ultimate depth of worthlessness was a plugged nickel. What this country needed was a good five-cent cigar. At a time when laborers

in New York made twenty cents an hour and a good meal would set you back fifteen cents, you could go into a saloon and, for a nickel, get a stein of beer and free bread, salami, pickled herring, and hard-boiled eggs for the asking. *"Barkeep, I'll have another beer."* When the subway opened up, naturally a ride was pegged at a nickel. This was the same as for streetcars, which particularly crisscrossed Brooklyn, so the players had to be nimble to negotiate streets to reach the ballpark: hence, the borough's team of Trolley Dodgers. The new movies not only charged a nickel, but were not called what they were, but what they cost: nickelodeons. A cuppa coffee cost a nickel. So did a soft drink. *"A Moxie, please." "Sure thing, mister, that'll be a nickel."* Ice cream was a nickel. Likewise a Tootsie Roll.

This single paragraph from the book *The Old Ball Game* stretches to 207 words, which, as a set piece, falls within our standards for short writing. I don't want to define focus in the way a Supreme Court justice once defined obscenity: "I know it when I see it." When I saw this paragraph for the first time, I knew it was focused. I could see, speak, and hear the feeling that all the parts of this paragraph were working in concert and that the author knew the one thing he wanted to say and then marshaled the evidence to support it.

The first sentence, "Uneeda knew pricing," serves as a transition from the previous sentence about the cost of a package of crackers. It is the next sentence that expresses the key point: "The nickel was king in America at this time." Take out the prepositional phrases, and you get the focus in four words: "The nickel was king."

Prove it! says the reader to herself. Show me!

And he does. I count eleven examples that coronate the currency, the first three embedded in familiar idioms of the day, and the next seven an inventory of things that cost five cents: a cigar, a beer, a movie, the subway, coffee, soda, ice cream, and candy. The passage is nailed tight with repetitions of the word *nickel*—ten in all.

David Von Drehle, an author and editor, won awards for his extraordinary writing on deadline. Deadline writing requires the sharpest focus, and Von Drehle would prepare himself to battle the clock with a set of focusing questions:

- Why does the story matter?
- What's the point?
- Why is the story being told?
- What does the story say about life, the world, the times we live in?

My colleague Chip Scanlan adds another question: What's my story really about?

It's the adverb *really* that matters. You could argue that a story by the magazine editor and author Jay Heinrichs is "about" his mother-in-law. Anna Jane has a serious heart condition and lies in a hospital bed, barely able to speak to loved ones gathered around to witness her dying.

Around 3 o'clock in the morning, Anna Jane lifted a weak finger and pointed to the can of Coke on a table across the room. "Sip o' that?" she whispered. So they propped her up and gave her a drink. She downed half the Coke, despite an oxymoronic nurse's protest that caffeine was bad for the dying woman. Three hours later Anna Jane was sitting up on her own; two days after that she checked out of the hospital, furious that she had failed to die on schedule. It took her a couple years before she finally joined her husband.

In other words, the doctors couldn't save her, but a Coke could.

What is the story *really* about? To me, it is about the good that can flow from the violation of conventional wisdom, which often calls for a challenge to authority. Perhaps the story is about Yogi Berra's baseball aphorism that "it ain't over till it's over."

In your reading and learning, you will recognize instances in which a text, even a short one, lacks focus. Consider these examples:

The topic is too wide: "Vandalism costs millions of dollars to repair." This is the equivalent of staring into a blue sky looking for a sliver of moon. Someone needs to help the writer answer questions that narrow the topic: What kind of vandalism? Exactly where in our community is this a problem? Can we find a microcosm, a single vandalized place that can stand for the others?

The author takes a detour: "Milli Vanilli was a German pop singing group in the late 1980s, a couple of pretty boys who preferred lip-synching to real singing, Germany being a place that produced several pop groups in that decade." The story of the defrocked boy band needs its own focus. The state of German pop music may be a useful piece of background, but here it's a distraction.

The writer lacks a sense of audience: The result is a confusion of language: "The Omega Point in human history illustrates a teleological perspective that can stretch like Bazooka bubble gum if you chew on it too long." I am one of those writers who like to allude to Saint Augustine of Hippo and the Hungry Hungry Hippos game in the same sentence. That verbal ventriloquism may mark my prose as edgy, but it will not matter if the work is unfocused.

Clutter hides a clear focus: "He was the kind of man who was way too busy to engage in common everyday activities, such as the flushing of toilets and the placing of dirty dishes in the dishwasher." (I've written a bloated version of the novelist Mona Simpson's great opening line "He was a man too busy to flush toilets.") Removal of clutter from a thirty-two-word sentence reveals a sharply focused lead sentence. Nine words outwork thirty-two. The shorter the text, the tighter the focus.

GRACE NOTES

1. Begin to notice in longer works paragraphs with a sharp focus. Save the best ones in your daybook.
2. Whatever you write, ask yourself the key questions:
   - What's my point?
   - In a sentence, what am I trying to say?
   - What is the work *really* about?

3. Test your short writing experiments with these additional questions:

- Have I taken a detour?
- Have I squeezed in extra stuff?
- Have I shifted tenses or language styles?

4. Examine earlier entries in your daybook with these questions:

- What is this bit really about?
- Can I answer that question in ten words? Five? Three?

4

Practice reading at a glance.

What happens when a reader can see a text all at once, without having to turn a page or scroll down the screen? You can hold a book and realize that it weighs a pound and includes six hundred pages or more. You may peek at the first page or the last, but you cannot see the entire text at a glance. When the text is short enough, you can have that experience. When you practice that single glance, you can begin to make predictions about how the reading will go. Here's what you can do:

- Make a quick decision about how long it will take to read the piece and whether the topic is worth your time.
- Notice the beginning, middle, and end all at the same time, helping you sense the logic of the whole.

- Spot interesting language, even before moving from first word to last, and make judgments about whether you are the best audience for this writer and this content.
- Experience the work within its setting, taking a variety of cues through accompanying elements such as photos, illustrations, typeface, design, or multimedia applications.

The at-a-glance experience is so valuable that writers and editors must take care not to undermine its effect. In other words, don't break up a small text into smaller texts. Make sure it is published—in total—on a single page or screen. Online, add links as you must, but don't clutter the text with so many opportunities to escape that the straight one-two-three meaning is lost.

Single-glance texts fulfill countless purposes, from the coupon to the soup label to the side panel of a cereal box to an advertising sign on the outfield wall.

Books are not, by definition, single-glance texts; but words on the front or back cover are. I'm staring now at the cover of Stieg Larsson's *The Girl Who Played with Fire,* the second volume of a trilogy of mystery thrillers, all now international best sellers. When I flip the book over, I see this marketing paragraph at a single glance:

Michael Blomkvist, crusading publisher of the magazine *Millennium,* has decided to run a story that will expose an extensive sex trafficking operation. On the eve of its publication, two people are brutally murdered, and the fingerprints found on the murder weapon belong to his friend, the troubled genius hacker Lisbeth Salander. Blomkvist, convinced of Salander's innocence, plunges into an investigation. Meanwhile, Salander herself is drawn into a murderous game of cat and mouse, which forces her to face her dark past.

Even the casual reader could finger the prefabricated phrases — *crusading publisher, expose, sex trafficking operation, brutally murdered, fingerprints found on the murder weapon, troubled genius hacker, plunges into, a murderous game, cat and mouse, face her dark past.* Such pulp-fiction patter may, like the clever carnival barker, attract an audience. But its pastiche of hyped clichés gives little evidence of what made Larsson's work so compelling and original.

Now I hold in my hand *The Last Boy: Mickey Mantle and the End of America's Childhood,* by Jane Leavy. On the cover is a photograph of the young center fielder for the New York Yankees, his face set in a Tom Sawyer grin. On the back cover I see five blurbs, testimony from a rich array of witnesses. The first comes from the historian Doris Kearns Goodwin:

> This is one of the best sports biographies I have ever read. Beautifully written and thoroughly researched, it reveals with stunning insight both the talents and the demons that drove Mickey Mantle, bringing him to life as never before.

That is stunning praise in thirty-nine words.

A complementary point of view comes from former Yankees manager Joe Torre:

> Every kid growing up in New York in the fifties wanted to be Mickey Mantle, including me. You wanted to wear the uniform like him, run like him, talk like him, look like him, and, most of all, play baseball like him. Jane Leavy has captured the hold he had on all of us in this gripping biography.

That one speaks right to me (I was one of those kids too, Joe) but it takes fifty-eight words. I'm starting to believe that a great blurb should be shorter, perhaps much shorter. So I reach for *The Hot Zone*, the nonfiction classic about a killer virus that stalks the human race. On the back is this blurb: "One of the most horrifying things I've ever read." Author? Stephen King. I think I just got a chill.

As a form of short writing, the blurb (or "advance praise," as it is euphemized in the business) is about a century old as a genre and has had a bit of feather duster clinging to it from the beginning. The name comes to us from a fictitious character, Miss Belinda Blurb, whose exaggerated praise was used to sell books and magazines. *Spy* magazine made fun of the practice as "logrolling in our time."

I love the practice. It's one of the only ways that friendly writers can help one another promote and sell their books. I love giving good blurbs and am even happier receiving them, such as this one from the humorist Dave Barry: "Roy Peter Clark knows more about writing than anyone I know who is not already dead." I have a feeling I will be using that one until I am actually dead, after which, who cares? The shorter the text—Barry's blurb is only sixteen words—the easier the at-a-glance experience.

GRACE NOTES

Try this experiment:

1. Select a short text from a newspaper or magazine, something that you can see at a glance. Do not read it word for word. Just give it a ten-second scan.

2. Write in your daybook a list of things you've learned just from the scan. Include predictions on what a more careful read will reveal.

3. Read the same text slowly, noting where your predictions came true or were frustrated.

4. Notice elements in and around the text that make it comprehensible at a glance:

- Key words in key locations
- Headlines or other directional language
- Navigational cues offered by the look of the page
- Punctuation, white space, type face and size

5

~~~

Follow the work of short writers.

I could not stop laughing after I wrote that title. It was just too bad to revise. I don't mean that you should follow the work of Alexander Pope, Søren Kierkegaard, Truman Capote, or Norman Mailer—writers who were short. Instead, I'm suggesting that you identify and follow the work of literary men and women known for their ability to write short texts with focus, wit, and polish.

I have read and reread about thirty of Shakespeare's plays and all the James Bond novels of Ian Fleming and all of J. K. Rowling and most of J. D. Salinger. We follow writers who have satisfied us, attracted as we may be to their stories, themes, and literary styles. Writers take this close attention to another level, distilling from the work the elements of craft that made it possible.

Apply that discipline to great short writing. When you

find a piece of good short writing, record the author's name ("poet William Carlos Williams") or the name of the feature (*"New Yorker*'s About Town") and begin to follow that work. Using testimony from the writer or careful analysis of texts, identify and adopt the methods of the best short writers.

Allow me to introduce to you my favorite short writer, who is actually of average height.

Let's imagine that in the year 2026 a spaceship, with humans aboard, lands on an asteroid or, better yet, crashes into a giant pockmarked space rock, the kind that once collided with Earth and flattened all our dinosaurs. All signals are cut off. The astronauts are presumed dead. It will take months for NASA to figure out what happened. It will issue a six-hundred-page report (with three thousand footnotes), and there will be fierce competition among media types to get the news out quickly, clearly, and accurately.

I'll put my money on Peter King, a correspondent for CBS Radio News, who has earned the reputation for being Johnny-on-the-spot for what is still called spot news. Simply stated, King has mastered the craft of distilling long, technical reports into ninety-second news updates. From his early days as a disc jockey, King was fitting sound and speech into strict time slots. He knew, for example, that he could play the long version of "Light My Fire" by the Doors, giving himself enough time to hit the bathroom and make another pot of coffee. Or, if he had just two minutes to fill, he could play "The Letter" by the Box Tops, at one minute and forty-six seconds the shortest number one hit of the rock-and-roll era.

As a correspondent, King knows that if he writes a report of one hundred words, it will take him thirty seconds to read it on the air, a calculation I call ART or approximate reading time. In order to take a 250-page NASA report on the disintegration of a space shuttle and translate it into a thirty-five-second breaking-news report for CBS Radio, King must be a quick study, able to boil down the story to its four-word essence, "The foam did it."

Such critical thinking enables the craft of short writing, and King has turned the reporting process into an exacting—some would say harsh—discipline. Here are his tips, strategies that you can practice, for writing short and fast and well:

- *Ask for help to understand what is technical and complex.* Scientific reports are hard to read because they are written for other scientists, some of whom are unwilling to "dumb down" their language for a mass audience. Look for the expert who shares a desire to hook up technical knowledge to the public good.

- *Select the most important piece of information to share with listeners.* Many experts and managers have testified that millions of dollars (or lives) can be lost because a crucial piece of information is buried in a long report. Like an archaeologist, the good writer can dig around and then dust off the hunk of gold that lies hidden beneath the surface.

- *Ask yourself, What information can I afford to leave out?* The jazz artist Miles Davis, along with many others, had to learn the art of leaving notes out. Silence—or white space—creates the canvas on which the best work can stand out for full appreciation.

- *Focus—that is, zero in.* Tight writing in all genres demands focus, that ability to get to the heart of the matter. Don't think reports or letters, King advises; think "picture postcard." Look for a single image to imprint on the mind of readers and listeners. Remember the ending of *King Kong*? "Oh no, it wasn't the airplanes. It was beauty killed the beast."

- *Select the best piece of something spoken, not the whole speech.* King would agree with the writing teacher Donald Murray's famous dictum that "brevity comes from selection and not compression." Caution: never rip the fragment from its context.

- *Create a shorthand, if necessary, to replace technical jargon.* As examples, King translates some of NASA's favorite abbreviations: EVA (extravehicular activity) = spacewalk; EMU (extravehicular mobility unit) = spacesuit; SRMS (shuttle remote manipulator system) = robot arm.

- *Search for and destroy redundant elements.* Adverbs are a favorite target, especially those that reinforce rather than modify the meaning of the verb, as in *totally severed* or *deeply rooted* or *curiously inquisitive.*

- *Apply the "What does it mean to me?" test.* "Would your mom, dad, aunt, or uncle understand?" asks King. But don't limit your sense of audience to family members alone. Would the bartender understand? Or your favorite nail technician? Or the hundred-dollar-an-hour plumber?

I was lucky enough to receive this great advice from Peter King in person, but what if he had died in 1959 and left no tactical counsel behind him? That was the case with Meyer Berger, perhaps the most versatile writer in the history of the *New York Times*. Among his accomplishments was the launching of the About New York column, which he maintained through most of the 1950s. Here is a short piece from April 20, 1953:

> The Waldorf-Astoria has its wine cellars, if you can call them that, on the fifth floor. The hotel is built on steel and concrete stilts, as most Park Avenue structures are that tower over the New York Central tracks. A stabilizer keeps the wine from being rocked by passing trains and other traffic.

Since I can't ask Berger to explain what he was trying to do, I must turn to the evidence of the work itself, which reveals those three key elements of great short writing: focus, wit, and polish. The focus is clear: preservation of expensive wine under shaky circumstances; the wit is revealed in the clever juxtaposition of the leisurely pleasures of wine consumption with a typical New York setting that jangles everyone's nerves; the polish takes advantage of the oxymoronic cellar on the fifth floor and renders the whole in fifty-three words.

Here is Berger again on the same day, under the label Marginalia:

> New York's subway cars and subway stations use left-hand threads in their electric-light bases. This discourages bulb snatchers from going after them for home use.

Berger proves he can go less than half the length of the adjoining piece, a quick study in the culture of bulb snatching and the bureaucracy prepared to thwart the perpetrators.

I have read almost everything that Berger wrote, including a book on the history of the *New York Times,* features he wrote for the *New Yorker,* the reconstruction of a mass murder that won him a Pulitzer, and a rich anthology of his short pieces. Not to get all Shakespearean on your collective asses, but writing does lend the author and subject a kind of immortality. Admire a living writer? Send an e-mail with a list of questions. A dead one? Put on your special X-ray glasses and study the work.

GRACE NOTES

1. If you find a writer of great short work, follow the writer over time.

2. If the writer has a website or a Facebook page or a Twitter account, ask to join.

3. Don't be afraid to ask writers specific questions about particular works or preferred writing strategies. Find out who and what the author is reading.

4. Check online booksellers to find the work of your favored writer. Consider the recommendations for authors who do similar work.

5. Remember the advice of Peter King:

- Ask for help in simplifying long, complicated material.
- Find the most important piece of information to share with readers.

- Decide what can be left out.
- Zero in.
- Excerpt the most telling quote.
- Translate jargon into common English.
- Search for and destroy redundancies.
- Play the role of the common reader.

6

Write in the margins.

I have on my shelf the first book I read at Providence College: *Dubliners,* a collection of short stories by James Joyce. It is the very book I purchased for $1.45 in September 1966 in the campus bookstore, a Compass Book published by the Viking Press.

Back then I wrote on the cover my name and my dorm room: Guzman 211. The green of the front cover has faded and the white of the back cover has yellowed with age. But the book is full of life for me. It is alive with words, images, and memories. It reminds me, most of all, of my greatest teacher: Rene Fortin.

Rene Fortin taught me how to read. That may seem like an odd thing to say; after all, I had brought a young life of avid reading with me to college. But Dr. Fortin, as we called him, challenged us to see the page—and through it, the world—in a new way.

"To be a real reader," he said, "you've got to mark up the page."

This may be the most important thing I've ever learned, and it seemed revolutionary at the time, even in the tumultuous era of the late 1960s. We had spent the last twelve years of our young lives learning that books were not our property. They belonged to the school. "If you write in these books," said one high school taskmaster, "your parents will be required to PAY for them."

In a single class, Dr. Fortin persuaded us that what we once thought of as vandalism—writing in books—was an indispensable tool of learning.

I find, in my awkward scribbles on the pages of *Dubliners,* an old treasure map of my learning, especially in the collection's final story, "The Dead." In this agonizingly poignant tale, a husband named Gabriel discovers, through the chance singing of an Irish ballad, that a young man, Michael Furey, died long ago for the love of Gabriel's wife.

I filled the margins of that story with brackets, check marks, and arrows. I underlined the words "westward" and "the palm of her glove." I marked off telling sentences, such as "Better pass boldly into that other world, in the full glory of some passion, than fade and wither dismally with age."

At the end of the story, I scribbled this about the husband Gabriel: "Wants to see that Distant Music is Irish Romance. He sees it in his wife. Mystery and Grace. Falls in love with wife and with the mystery of the young man." By the second semester, focusing on modern poetry, I was marking up texts with a passion: circling key words, sketching patterns of language, finding meaning in the margins.

To learn the craft of short writing, begin to think of marginalia as a genre. It will help to remember that writing in the margins is for an audience of one—the writer. The purpose is not publication but learning, thinking, analyzing, discovering, and remembering. But marginalia has been uncovered and studied, sometimes in the work of distinguished authors and scholars. The most famous of these even has a name: Fermat's conjecture.

Pierre de Fermat was a French mathematician, a brilliant scholar and lawyer who made many lasting contributions to the formal study of numbers. But none of them became as famous—or infamous—as a bit of unfinished business that began as nothing more than marginalia. The year was 1637, and Fermat was reading an ancient Greek text called *Arithmetica,* written by a third-century numbers guy named Diophantus. Something in the text tickled Fermat's imagination, moving him to jot this note in the margins, translated from the Latin: "It is impossible to separate a cube into two cubes, or a fourth power into two fourth powers, or in general, any power higher than the second, into two like powers. I have discovered a truly marvelous proof of this, which this margin is too narrow to contain."

Too narrow to contain!

It appears that Fermat never got on with the task of sharing his "truly marvelous proof," and number nerds spent more than three centuries to seal the deal. In 1994 an English brainiac, Andrew John Wiles, turned Fermat's conjecture into his last theorem and took only one hundred pages to do so.

Wouldn't it be great to have Hemingway's original edition of Mark Twain's *The Adventures of Huckleberry Finn*? How about Sylvia Plath's personal copy of *The Great Gatsby*? It exists in a South Carolina library and offers wonderful insights into the mind of a young poet. It is not known whether Plath read Fitzgerald in high school or college, but her underlines and marginalia reveal an active and creative young mind. The most compelling is a note on a scene in which Tom and Daisy Buchanan are spotted through a window of their house as Gatsby walks up their driveway. Plath wrote: "knight waiting outside—dragon goes to bed with princess."

The website of the University of South Carolina library comments that "with this note Plath's annotation rises from mundane commentary to incisive interpretation. Many of Plath's later poems employ fairy-tale allusions, usually with the inverted imagery she employs here."

Writing in the margins of books is a way of trying things out.

I threw away all my term papers from college and graduate school, but I have uncovered a map of my mind in the margins of the textbooks I have saved to this day. I had an affinity for poems about carnal love or spiritual love—or both, which led me to the work of the seventeenth-century poet John Donne. "The Canonization," for example, is a forty-five-line poem in which the narrator fends off his friends and begs them to "let me love." While this is not the moment for a full explication, I can show you what I was thinking about it in 1968. In my notes I underline, circle, or bracket twenty-three words or passages. Check out what I scribbled in the margins:

- Petrarch
- Reconcile all opposites
- Man—woman—reason—femininity
- Movement from insignificance to significance
- Through the movement from a fly to a phoenix
- Eagle—traditional symbol of reason flies into the sun
- Fly—taper both have short existence
- Taper—funeral, insignificant, self-destructive
- Phoenix—symbol of sex act
- Stanza—room
- Legend—life of saint
- Sonnets—immortality
- Neutral—two things are one
- Continue to exist
- Beg from above—asking them to intercede

Through the mirror of these markings, I recognize myself as a student learning to read the text closely in the tradition of what was called the New Criticism. These marks would lead to a piece of writing, an interpretation of the poem. But that is just the aftermath. The main work is in my head and in the margins of the text.

GRACE NOTES

1. Never read a newspaper, magazine, or book without a pen nearby. You already "talk back" to the author and text—at least in your mind. Get in the habit of writing those thoughts in the margins of the page.

2. After you've finished reading a work, do a quick review of your marginal notes. Use your daybook to continue the "conversation" with the author or to summarize your own arguments.

3. If you own an e-book reader, experiment with the notes mode to create the equivalent of marginalia.

4. Next time you are in a bookstore that sells used books, search to find some golden oldies in which an owner of a book (or more than one!) talks back to the author in the margins.

5. Search on the Internet for "marginalia" and write briefly on what you discover.

7

~~~

Embrace the lyric.

There may be no more efficient form of short writing than the song lyric. The words do not stand alone, of course. They have plenty of company. A melody and repetition of sounds make the words memorable. The lyrics often tell a story. That story can be rendered in a music video or through a dramatic stage performance. The song may be used to help score a movie. Written for an opera, for example, the lyrics become part of a multimedia extravaganza, the effect—as in Verdi—of which is to capture and express an entire national artistic culture. Cue the elephants.

Many great lyrics are taken for granted and not appreciated as poetry in their own right. A few lyrics deserve the close reading we might apply to higher forms of art, such as a poem by Ezra Pound. To test this theory, I will interpret the lyrics of a Tom Petty song, "Free Falling" (sometimes rendered "Free Fallin'"). I've played its three chords on guitar and piano and have tried to sing its lyrics of 150 words, although I can't hit Petty's high notes. I find these lyrics haunting, profound through and beneath the surface of sound. Most important for our purposes, this piece of short writing is efficient beyond measure, so economical, in fact, that it leads us to the edge of a great abyss.

> She's a good girl, loves her mama
> Loves Jesus and America too
> She's a good girl, crazy 'bout Elvis
> Loves horses and her boyfriend too

Stories have few essential requirements, but one of them involves the identification and evolution of a human character, formed on the page by a quilt of what Tom Wolfe called "status details," or, more commonly, character traits. Petty doesn't offer us much in his first stanza in the way of particularity. He asks us to settle for a litany of common, almost clichéd characteristics. God, mother, horses, form a kind of baseline, drawn, as we will learn, by a greatly flawed narrator, another staple of modern fiction.

The half line that gets me every time—so much so that I appear to hear it above the rest—is "crazy 'bout Elvis." She could love the Beatles or the Byrds but chooses Elvis to love, a bad boy in his own right, whose addictions will lead to an early grave. Think of the phrase "crazy 'bout Elvis" as a kind of grace note—that is, a small, almost exquisite ornament in music, most surprising when it turns out to be the only decoration.

It's a long day livin' in Reseda
There's a freeway runnin' through the yard
And I'm a bad boy, 'cause I don't even miss her
I'm a bad boy for breakin' her heart

A story needs a setting, and this one serves in both literal and symbolic ways. Poets know that place-names are powerful, and Reseda, a working-class suburb of Los Angeles, has the sound of "receding" in it, a kind of annihilation by subtraction. That freeway runs a little too close for comfort. Usually, the poorest folks in town live closest to the highway or the airport or the railroad tracks, a kind of lifeline to freedom that remains inaccessible. Just below the surface here is the joke that California is so cluttered with people and traffic that the freeway is not free at all but a clotted artery of the body politic, a society all revved up but going nowhere. That last line reverberates with some kind of dark humor and self-effacement, as Petty leads a great band known as the Heartbreakers.

And I'm free, I'm free fallin', fallin'

In this simple chorus, Petty puts into play some very sophisticated moves, both poetically and musically. I experience it as a form of binary energy, an on/off switch, a double helix of language in which the words alliterate, form connections, but then break away at the level of semantics and narrative. A free fall is a common expression of physical weightlessness, a state in physics and art where an object or person seems to defy gravity even while plummeting to the ground. Petty, quite dramatically, puts his vocal range to good use, hitting his highest note on the elongated vowel of "free." But each time he repeats "fallin'," the notes go down in pitch.

> All the vampires walkin' through the valley
> Move west down Ventura Blvd.
> And all the bad boys are standing in the shadows
> All the good girls are home with broken hearts

This is my favorite stanza, linked and separated by alliteration. The first quartet includes "vampires," "valley," "Ventura," and even "Blvd.," where those *v*'s pile up like crashed cars in a smoky fog. There is even time and space here for what the critics call intertextuality, the evocation of one text by another. "Though I walk through the valley of the shadow of death," reads the Twenty-Third Psalm, but here the allusion packs some irony. Instead of comforting and consoling, the world of the narrator is gloomy and tragic, haunted by the walking dead of the San Fernando Valley.

> And I'm free, I'm free fallin'
>
> I wanna glide down over Mulholland
> I wanna write her name in the sky
> I wanna free fall out into nothin'
> Gonna leave this world for a while

In this final stanza the voice of the narrator tells a story of despair, of drug use or suicide perhaps, of escape from responsibility and the requirements of love. And yet the diction is a language of light, those liquid *l* sounds in "glide" and "Mulholland," the creativity and romance signified by skywriting, but then comes the nihilism of "free fall out into nothin'" and the painful euphemism of leaving the world "for a while." We can make the interpretation of this text even more granular in the tension between the names of those iconic California streets, Ventura and Mulholland. If that initial capital *V* looks like a valley, with all its symbolic connotations of depression and despair, that *M* is its counterpart, two mountain peaks with a valley in the middle, a launching place in the hills above Hollywood, a land of dreams and of lost boys and girls.

And I'm free, I'm free fallin'...

GRACE NOTES

Consider the lessons we can draw from such an analysis of song lyrics. What practices and language moves can we apply to our own writing?

- Use simple words to build dramatic ideas.
- Depend on characters, conflict, scenes, setting, and narrators, no matter how short the story form.
- In music and writing, use repetition to hold narrative and thematic elements together, as in a chain, and make them memorable.
- Use a short text to remind readers of other short texts, enriching the experience of narrative.
- Remember that literal language benefits from its coexistence with figurative words, from metaphors to literary allusions to sound imagery to symbolism and more.

8

~~~

No dumping.

Have you ever seen a No Dumping sign next to a field or wooded area? If you don't have the guts to steal one, perhaps you can use a photo as one of your screen savers. "No dumping" is not a bad motto for how to write well on the Internet, especially if you want to master the shortest of the short forms of writing.

When I think of writers such as the versatile Stephanie Hayes of the *Tampa Bay Times* and Jay Rosen, a scholar and critic who blogs at PressThink, I am reminded that they share, in spite of their many differences, one essential writing value: unlike other writers, they never dump stuff online. I get the impression, reinforced by conversations with both, that they revise their writing online — no matter how short — with the same rigor they would bring to editing the chapters of a book.

I first encountered the concept of notes dumping from a

reporter with high standards whose editor told him about the importance of both writing short and being first on competitive news stories. In a nanosecond news cycle, argued the editor, the reporter must overcome traditional inhibitions and get content on the paper's website almost as soon as it has been gathered. Content, his editor said, can be corrected, updated, enhanced, and revised in later versions. For now, "just dump your notes."

Text messaging and instant messaging, for example, are well known for their word-dump informality, filled as they are with the acronymic, emoticonic alphabet soup that characterizes the license-plate language coding of the Internet:

MOM: Where u at?
DAUGHTER: With Rob J nxt 2 bleachers
MOM: Rt after game. Be at 1st St. exit
DAUGHTER: U drivin da tank?
MOM: Stealin' dad's Caddy!!!

In such a language environment, what should be the level of language for use on social networks? It depends, in part, on whether you use Facebook and Twitter for personal or professional reasons. It also depends on your purpose and your intended audience. To express congratulations, your tone can be playful. To express condolences, you'll probably want to slip on that plain gray suit. But here is the key: whether the writing is formal or informal, whether it appears as a tome or a paragraph, the writer has the duty to perfect, polish, and revise, even if that work needs to be done in a minute or less.

Jay Rosen uses social networks to reach and expand the

audience for his ideas on politics, culture, technology, and news. His more than seventy thousand followers on Twitter have become familiar with his writing voice, which I would describe as assertively conversational. Here is one of his tweets:

> That the re-design is always hated by regular users led designers to the odd conclusion that there's no such thing as a hateful re-design.

And another:

> The three replies I get the most to my Twitter posts: 1) And this surprises you because...? 2) There's nothing new in that 3) "Not always."

To each of these, Rosen attaches a link where the reader can find the original source, a generous act unto itself, and one that the Internet was designed to perform. But I remain interested in Rosen's own prose and the way, in spite of its brevity, it reveals a curious and governing intelligence. These sentences are not dumped, readers; they are crafted.

Let's take a piece of short writing by Rosen that appears on his blog PressThink:

> Today we say media instead of "the press." But it's a mistake. The press has become the ghost of democracy in the media machine, and we need to keep it alive.

Looking through the rhetorical machinery of these three short sentences, it's intriguing to see the Rosen ghost haunting it. The simple language is deceiving in that it expresses an intellectual distinction. In short, the media are one thing. The press (or journalism) is another. They should not be confused. And look at the work accomplished by the layered allusions to "the ghost in the machine." You may recognize it as the title of a music album by the group the Police. Or as the title of Arthur Koestler's 1967 book and its attack on B. F. Skinner. Or you may be as smart as Rosen and recognize.the phrase as the work of the philosopher Gilbert Ryle and his attack on mind/body dualism.

You get the same intelligence working through Rosen's Twitter posts:

> What happens when a community loses its newspaper? [Link] I think it depends on what died: "the" newspaper or "our" newspaper.

Or

> To Elizabeth Murdoch and her husband [Rupert], "striking out on your own" means starting a company with dad's money [Link]. Not kidding.

You will encounter a different voice in the work of Stephanie Hayes, whose writing—in fiction, reporting, or fashion criticism—sounds hip and connected. She writes on Facebook: "Will I ever get tired of Bridget Jones? Do I have some neural receptor blockage thing that makes it amazing every time?" Or "I'm going cold turkey off diet Coke for a week starting tomorrow. In related news, cross me and I'll cut you."

Hayes's posts are brainy in their own way, but also youthful, playful, personal, and self-deprecating. Here is a sample from Twitter:

> To the girl driving frantically with a head full of Velcro rollers: I feel you.

Or

> Few things are more chilling than a fleet of trucks on the highway carrying portable toilets.

Or

> Just got a press kit in the mail from Gallo with a wine cork marked "starter cork." They obviously don't know me.

The voice sounds like the same writer, even though the-purpose of each message is different, from a sympathetic social observation about young women on the go, to a scatological psychodrama in the making, to the confessions of an experienced sinner. No matter how personal and casual her posts may seem on a first read, they always, upon further review, show the effects of crafting, not dumping.

GRACE NOTES

1. Place a sign on or near your computer: No Dumping.

2. Make a list of the informal texts you would be least likely to revise: e-mails, tweets, status updates, website feed-

back, instant messages. Resolve that for one week you will refrain from dumping these on your readers and will take a few seconds to correct and improve.

3. Remember that great writing in an informal style is the product of a set of formal practices, including the intentional deletion of function words; the use of contractions and other abbreviations; and the employment of slang, dialect, and other idioms.

4. Review the excerpts from the writings of Jay Rosen and Stephanie Hayes. Write a brief analysis of each, with attention to evidence of focus, wit, and polish.

9

⚡

Tap the power of two.

The most basic move in short writing is the *one-two punch*. At the levels of phrase, sentence, paragraph, and short essay, the author takes two elements of language and rubs them together for effect. Even in the shortest of texts, there has to be a little rub. No rub means no friction. No friction means no spark. With no spark, there can be no fire, no illumination. Rub, friction, spark, fire, light—all these derive from the power of two.

I've long taught that three was the magic number in writing, the digit that symbolized wholeness, fullness, the total package. But in an accelerating world, it appears that the power of two is catching up. The one-two punch rules the double helix of genetics and the zero/one calculations of computer science as well as many other cultural expressions:

Yin/yang
On/off
Concave/convex
Conflict/resolution
Bass/treble
Yankees/Red Sox

Such dualities are ancient and enduring. In fast times, they manifest themselves not only on the theoretical but also on the granular level, making decisions more urgent—even in writing.

To explore the origins and potential of the one-two punch, consider a standard genre of English composition class, writing an essay in which you compare and contrast two things, conditions, or issues. I recall that my wife and three daughters fulfilled this assignment during their early college years by discussing in four different essays the relative merits of breast versus bottle feeding. The breast always won!

While useful, such assignments put the cart before the horse—and then demand that the horse push the cart up the hill with its nose. You can't write a good sonnet until you know how it feels to brim with love. You can't write a good one-two essay until confronted with a real problem and two competing solutions.

Before his untimely death, my college friend James Slevin had become one of America's most influential writing scholars and was just as good, if not better, in the classroom. We sat in the basement of his parents' house on Long Island one evening, drinking beers and talking about teaching. Jim picked up a yellow pad and drew a simple cross, filling up the page, with the crossbar near the top.

"We ask students to perform these tasks," he said to me, "without demonstrating for them the tools we all need to complete them. Anytime I'm trying to compare and contrast some competing ideas, the first thing I do is to create this diagram."

Atop each column he would write the two elements being compared and contrasted. Today they could be the Tea Party versus the Occupy Wall Street movements. Or Young Adults with Health Insurance versus Ones Without. Or Literary Memoir versus Journalistic Memoir. Or Madonna versus Lady Gaga.

Since Jim shared that simple tool with me, I've spent more than three decades making distinctions, rendered in a one-two structure. What is the difference, for example, between a report and a story? The purpose of the report, I argued, was to deliver information so that readers could act on it. A story, on the other hand, was a form of vicarious experience. A report might *point* you there, but a story *puts* you there. To illustrate, I listed, side by side, the reporting and writing strategies inherent in each of them. A report, for example, requires us to find out who was involved; in a story there is a special name for the who. We call it a character. The result of such thinking was this chart:

Report	*Story*
Who	Character
What	Scene (what happened)

When	Chronology (time in motion)
Where	Setting
Why	Motive
How	Process

I could construct an essay—even a book—by following these parallel themes. But the invitation to compare and contrast can also come in granular form, either as an element in a text or as a tightly focused piece of short writing, such as the following:

> The purpose of the report is to *point* you there, but the story *puts* you there. To understand that difference, the writer need only translate the basic elements of the report into elements of narrative, so that Who becomes Character; What becomes Scene; Where becomes Setting; When becomes Chronology; Why becomes Motive; and How becomes Process, or how it happened. (60 words)

To test the elements of the one-two punch, I decided to identify a topic I had not written about before. It came to me in an argument over the way black performing artists were exploited by white producers and performers, especially in the 1950s, when race in America was a powder keg and rock music was emerging from the South. The classic case pits two successful but wildly different artists: Little Richard, who helped invent rock music with songs like "Tutti Frutti" and "Long Tall Sally," and Pat Boone, who sang cover versions in an effort to neutralize the effects of what was dubbed "race music" for white audiences. Consider these two:

Little Richard Penniman	*Pat Boone*
Black	White
Gay	Straight
Wild	Mild
Dirty and flirty	Squeaky clean
Originator	Duplicator
Dangerous	Safe
Icon	Has-been

Armed with these persuasive elements of contrast, I am ready to write a little something:

> Bleach is for more than laundry or hair. You can bleach a culture, too, robbing it of its color, its energy, its soul. It happened the first time I heard the song "Tutti Frutti" performed by a straight, white, squeaky-clean imitator named Pat Boone. The emptiness of his version became clear only when I was exposed to the original performed by Little Richard Penniman, a wild, pompadoured, dirty, flirty brother, whose screeches and wails tested every taboo that 1950s white America had to offer. (85 words)

With lots of work, I would hope my essay could be as compelling and clever as this one-paragraph 1964 essay by John Updike, titled "Beer Can":

> This seems to be an era of gratuitous inventions and negative improvements. Consider the beer can. It was beautiful—as beautiful as the clothespin, as inevitable as the

wine bottle, as dignified and reassuring as the fire hydrant. A tranquil cylinder of delightfully resonant metal, it could be opened in an instant, requiring only the application of a handy gadget freely dispensed by every grocer. Who can forget the small, symmetrical thrill of those two triangular punctures, the dainty *pfff*, the little crest of suds that foamed eagerly in the exultation of release? Now we are given, instead, a top beetling with an ugly, shmoo-shaped tab, which, after fiercely resisting the tugging, bleeding fingers of the thirsty man, threatens his lips with a dangerous and hideous hole. However, we have discovered a way to thwart Progress, usually so unthwartable. *Turn the beer can upside down and open the bottom.* The bottom is still the way the top used to be. True, this operation gives the beer an unsettling jolt, and the sight of a consistently inverted beer can might make people edgy, not to say queasy. But the latter difficulty could be eliminated if manufacturers would design cans that looked the same whichever end was up, like playing cards. What we need is Progress with an escape hatch. (*New Yorker*, January 18, 1964)

I've always admired this essay, perhaps because it was written near the time I began my own experiments with beer guzzling, so I very much remember the invention of the pop-top as both a practical ("Hey, this is cool") and an unaesthetic ("Man, that's ugly") object. We had a euphemistic name for Updike's "handy gadget freely dispensed by every grocer." Back in the day, we called it a church key.

On the level of craft, notice Updike's economy, how much

he derives from a one-two punch of comparison/contrast—all done in an efficient 218 words. It begins with the author standing atop a level of abstraction. We live in an era of gratuitous inventions and (the oxymoronic) negative improvements. Do we really, John? What made you think of that? Can you show us an example? Anticipating such questions, he dives off his abstraction to the object of his worship and scorn: the beer can.

What follows is classic comparison/contrast, beginning with a list of wonderful attributes of the old can. It is beautiful, tranquil, reassuring, dignified, delightful, resonant, handy, instantaneous, thrilling, symmetrical, dainty, eager, exultant in its foamy ejaculation.

But that was then, a golden age of beer drinking. Now we have an innovation associated with pejorative language. The pop-top is beetling, ugly, shmoo-shaped. It resists the drinker, nay, makes his fingers bleed, and threatens his lips with hideous, unspeakable danger.

So far, the author's one-two punch moves the reader from abstract to concrete, from general to specific, from a litany of love to one of disgust, from the romanticism of the old to the skepticism of the new. But Updike is not yet finished because he has another binary movement to make, from problem to solution. How will we thwart Progress (a generality)? By pragmatism: turn the beer can upside down. In those days, the bottom was like the old top, but this would cause some collateral damage unless design rushes to our rescue, giving us a can that looks the same upside down, like a playing card. Updike's resolution brings the abstract/concrete move back full circle, in the form of a moral lesson: we need Progress with an escape hatch.

In its original form in the *New Yorker* magazine, Updike's essay looked a little like a beer can. And then there is the shape and logic of the essay itself:

Abstract problem
Specific example
List of positives
List of negatives
Specific solution
Abstract lesson

If I didn't know better—and I don't—it appears as if the architecture of this one-two essay works so that you could turn it upside down and it would look almost the same, whichever end was up.

GRACE NOTES

1. Create a one-two chart—like the ones described above—for Updike's essay "Beer Can." Atop the left column write "Old Can," and on the right, "New Can." Starting with "Ugly" versus "Beautiful," fill out the chart using Updike's elements.

2. Write a short essay in imitation of Updike. You can even begin it the same way—with a tweak. "We live in an era of gratuitous inventions and negative improvements. Consider _____." Fill in the blank.

3. In your reading, begin to notice examples of comparison/contrast and other literary and cultural dualities. Keep a list in your daybook.

10

◥◥◥

Learn to balance.

I watched an old movie recently, set in the 1950s, in which Henny Youngman, the so-called king of the one-liners, makes a cameo appearance. In front of a nightclub audience, he delivers his famous opening joke: "Take my wife, please." And then another: "I take my wife everywhere, but she always finds her way home."

The next day I received in the mail a copy of the thin volume *Signposts to Elsewhere*, a collection of aphorisms written by the Arab author Yahia Lababidi. As I flipped through the book, these examples of very short writing caught my eye:

- "The small spirit is quick to misperceive an insult, the large spirit is slow to receive a compliment."
- "Opposites attract, similarities last."
- "A day is a lifetime, and a lifetime a day."

Not all the author's examples are written in this balanced one-two structure, just enough so that the power and versatility of the move become apparent. It can be used by a Jewish comedian or an Arabic philosopher.

It is not enough to call the one-two move the most effective and common strategy for writing short. There are, happily, a few variations that deserve special attention, useful examples with their own names. By way of introduction, let's call these moves *balanced, unbalanced, change of pace,* and *hitting the target.*

The *balanced* move is best exemplified by a famous catchphrase spoken by Muhammad Ali as a young boxer: "Float like a butterfly, sting like a bee." This compound sentence (made up of two equally important main clauses) balances like a seesaw on the pivot of that comma and gains extra strength from its parallel structure, equal syntactical units to express meaning of equal weight. The mirror images go like this: imperative verb, preposition, article, noun. Even with all this, the two halves aren't precisely equal. The difference between *butterfly* and *bee*—the first word long and lyrical, the second short and sharp—creates both rhythm and contrast. Ali is both the beauty and the beast.

Such balance is not limited to the level of phrase or sentence. It can work at the paragraph level as well. Take this example written by the illustrator Lou Beach in the form of a 420-character social network update:

> I've never seen who lives across the street in the house with the peeling paint, broken steps. The shades are always down and the mailman rarely stops there, no

paper is delivered. Only in winter is there any sign of activity. Every day the snow behind the chainlink fence is peppered with birdseed and the yard is alive with sparrows and finches, chickadees and dark-eyed juncos.

You can almost measure the balance in that vignette of sixty-six words. The first two sentences total thirty-two words and present details of alienation and lifelessness. The house itself, like Poe's House of Usher, is in a state of decay. No one seems to be taking care of it, just as no one makes any effort to connect with the world outside. Except in winter, when we might expect the place to be even more desolate. But whoever is in exile inside that house cares enough for the birds to provide the seed they need to make it through the hard season.

We can begin the search for new examples of the balanced move in *The World According to Twitter*, by David Pogue, and *Twitter Wit*, edited by Nick Douglas.

- "Discovered today that Costco sells caskets. For $799 my bachelor pad just got a bit more interesting." (@snc)
- "Ran out of deodorant midway, so one arm is Shower Fresh, the other is Eastern Lily. This has the makings of a wild day." (@phillygirl)
- "The baby just saw me naked. Now she knows where she got her thighs." (@AuntMarvel)

The following are drawn from the anthology *Hint Fiction,* stories written with a twenty-five-word limit, edited by Robert Swartwood.

- "She placed her hand over his and pressed the pen to paper. The signature looked shaky, but it should be enough." (Katrina Robinson, "Visiting Hours")
- "Sleeping Beauty never minded the spindle prick. It was the wake-up kiss she hated." (Val Gryphin, "Insomnia")
- "He was allergic. She pretended not to know." (Camille Esses, "Peanut Butter")

I find it most encouraging as a writer to find ancient rhetorical strategies of short writing repurposed for use in our most modern forms of discourse and most advanced media platforms.

GRACE NOTES

1. A compound sentence is made up of two or more clauses of equal weight, each of which could stand as a simple sentence. "Willie Mays hit more home runs than Mickey Mantle" is a simple sentence. I can add this clause: "but Mantle was widely recognized as the more powerful slugger." Together they form a compound sentence: "Willie Mays hit more home runs than Mickey Mantle, but Mantle was widely recognized as the more powerful slugger." Notice the balance between the two ideas, a perfect vehicle for comparison and contrast.

2. The one-two structure works on the textual or global level, from a book title such as *The Glamour of Grammar* to a book on global warming, organized by problem and

solution. Begin to look for balanced examples in your reading, especially in shorter forms such as tweets.

3. In a paragraph of about sixty words, imitate the one-two structure demonstrated in the example by Lou Beach. As a guide, make sure a sentence ends near the middle, so that you can create a second part for a balanced effect.

11

⚡

Give weight to one side.

Let's turn now to the subordinating or *unbalanced* move, a strategy that takes advantage of the complex, rather than the compound, sentence structure. I found an example among the Wit & Wisdom selections chosen for the December 23, 2011, edition of the *Week* magazine. "When all else fails," said the Israeli diplomat Abba Eban, "men turn to reason." One can easily detect a numerical balance in the two clauses, each executed in just four words. But the meanings are not in balance. The first clause is adverbial and cannot stand alone. The key is in that second clause, the one that defines human beings as rational animals, even in moments of crisis.

Let's review the basics. The complex sentence creates a one-two imbalance, making one clause in a sentence dependent on another. The stronger clause is often called the *main* or *independent* clause because it can stand by itself as a Standard English sentence. Together the strong and weak elements act like a parent and a child on a seesaw. The child, of lesser weight, depends on the grown-up for all the energy and control.

In an unbalanced sentence, the main clause can come either before or after the subordinate clause. This can offer readers slightly different effects. Opening with the weaker clause offers some suspense, since the reader must wait till the end of the sentence to grasp the main meaning: "When I get home from work," says the mother, "I'll check your homework," or "I'll have a special treat for you."

In short writing, the subordinate clause will often come at or near the beginning of a sentence, establishing the conditions for the main idea: "When one of us is chained, none of us are free." But the parts can be reversed, often to good effect, as when the British author Virginia Woolf offered this wisdom to an American journalist: "One cannot think well, love well, sleep well, if one has not dined well."

Though it may be harder to detect in more formal writing or speech, subordination becomes a crucial element in the construction of an argument. For proof of this we need look no further than the first sentence of the Declaration of Independence:

> When in the Course of human events, it becomes necessary for one people to dissolve the political bands which have connected them with another, and to assume among the powers of the earth, the separate and equal station to which the Laws of Nature and of Nature's God entitle

them, a decent respect to the opinions of mankind requires that they should declare the causes which impel them to the separation.

In a shorter and less formal version, it might go something like, "When people want to break away from one government and form their own, it makes sense to list their reasons for doing so." Here are more examples:

- "When in doubt," said the mystery writer Raymond Chandler, "have two guys come through the door with guns."
- "If you can't annoy somebody," said the British novelist Kingsley Amis, "there is little point in writing."
- "When walking through a melon patch," reads a Chinese proverb, "don't adjust your sandals."
- "While you're saving your face," reported President Lyndon Johnson, "you're losing your ass."
- "If you have a job without aggravations," said the business tycoon Malcolm Forbes, "you don't have a job."
- "If you live in New York, even if you're Catholic, you're Jewish." This last one, my favorite, came from the comedian Lenny Bruce, who uses not one but two subordinate clauses.

I found those six examples simply by flipping through the pages of the Robert Byrne collection *The 2,548 Best Things Anybody Ever Said.*

Here are examples of the unbalanced move found on Twitter:

- "When your feelings are best described by a Jewel song, it's probably time to hide the cutlery." (@srslainey)
- "If someone spits gum on the sidewalk, we should be able to take their DNA from it, clone them, and beat the shit out of their clone." (@paulfeig)
- "When the moon hits your eye like a big pizza pie, that's both astronomically and opthalmologically catastrophic." (@MikeTRose)

GRACE NOTES

1. In his book *The Alphabet Versus the Goddess,* Leonard Shlain quotes the first Mesopotamian written law, circa 2350 BC, in which the legislator makes use of the unbalanced move: "If a woman speaks out against her man, her mouth shall be crushed with a hot brick." Using examples from the last two chapters as models, experiment in your daybook with both the balanced and the unbalanced moves.

2. Here are three balanced sentences that connect two or more independent clauses. Create some imbalance by making at least one clause subordinate to the others. For example, "It was a sixty-degree day in February, and the citizens of Iowa came out to play" becomes something like "When it hits sixty degrees in February, Iowans will abandon their snowsuits and come out to play." Have fun with these examples.

- The ballerina was determined to stick to her diet, but then she heard the bells of the ice cream truck.

- The sun sank below the horizon; a pair of dolphins jumped in the Gulf; Tom and Mildred headed for the bar.
- Politicians always try to convince you that their origins are humble; lots of pols live in million-dollar mansions.

12

~~~

Change your pace.

The *change-of-pace* (or *long/short*) move requires a passage of at least two sentences. In the clearest example, it begins with one or more sentences of significant length, followed by a short sentence or fragment that acts almost as a form of end punctuation. It's as if the momentum from the long sentences needs something more than a period (or full stop) to bring it to a screeching halt. It needs a word or phrase. Try this example, written as a Facebook update, by the visual artist Lou Beach:

> The beautiful young woman waves at me across the plaza. I wave back and approach her, realize too late that she was waving at the man behind me. I open my mouth to speak as they embrace, kiss, and look deep into each other's eyes. I stand alone, surrounded by the festive crowd, feel

old and foolish. I buy a postcard to send to my wife and children in Ohio. "Having a great time. Wish you were her."

What a darkly humorous inversion of the postcard cliché "Wish you were *here*." Whether it is intentional or a Freudian slip, those last four words act like the windshield of a car ignoring the speed limit. The author better wear a seat belt because when he slams on the brakes, all the forces of inertia threaten to propel him through the glass.

Norman O. Brown gets into the act, writing in *Love's Body* about breaking the rules of language:

> Freedom is poetry, taking liberties with words, breaking the rules of normal speech, violating common sense. Freedom is violence.

For the record, that aphorism begins with a rolling sentence of sixteen words that runs into a fence of three words. Here he goes longer:

> Psychoanalysis began as a further advance of civilized (scientific) objectivity; to expose remnants of primitive participation, to eliminate them; studying the world of dreams, of primitive magic, of madness, but not participating in dreams or magic, or madness. But the outcome of psychoanalysis is the discovery that magic and madness are everywhere, and dreams [are] what we are made of. The goal cannot be the elimination of magical thinking, or madness; the goal can only be conscious magic, or

conscious madness; conscious mastery of these fires. And dreaming while awake.

This final phrase works for Brown on many levels: on the rhythmic level, bringing the song to a close; on the content level, serving to summarize or conclude; on the visual level, acting as a tidy fence to prevent the garden of words from overgrowing its allotted boundaries.

As we've seen several times now, great pieces of short writing can be extracted from much longer pieces. The rhythmic move of long/short works well at the paragraph level, especially in long essays and books, where it can be used to control the momentum of the reader. Notice how Leonard Shlain turns the trick in the book *The Alphabet Versus the Goddess,* a study of the tension in Western culture between the image and the written word. The example refers to Martin Luther and controversies over the worship of idols:

> Luther thought that imagery might be useful in teaching the illiterate. The students, nobles, townspeople, and peasants who were electrified by his message, however, did not share his generous attitude about images. As happened during the first three protestant reformations, zealots wielding sledge-hammers and pickaxes smashed statues, slashed paintings, and upended altarpieces. Priests or parishioners who tried to protect these images were stoned or beaten. Artists fled.

To understand the deceleration of this passage, just plot out sentence length: 11, 21, 21, 13, 2. As a rule of thumb, the more periods there are in a passage, the slower the reader will move, since each period is a stop sign. You can see how the reader builds momentum in those two long sentences but then must slow down with a significantly shorter sentence and then a final two-word barricade that pops out of the slowing spacecraft like a parachute.

It is even possible to change the pace in the 140 characters allowed by Twitter, as revealed in these tweets drawn from *The World According to Twitter* and *Twitter Wit:*

- "Southwest flight attendant held up seatback card during safety demo. Colleague had written, 'I need a man' on it. Whole plane laughing." (@DavidBThomas)
- "My girlfriend in high school came to where I was working to collect her hair scrunchie I kept on the shifter in my car. I knew it was over." (@bnl771)
- "Wife, playing Scrabble with mom, looking over her letters, realizing: 'Jujitsu. I can spell Jujitsu.' She's the Neo of Word Nerds." (@tj)

If you read such examples aloud, you hear a kind of rhythm, an effect created when the writer adjoins sentences of different lengths.

GRACE NOTES

Read the following excerpt from the photo book *Old Dogs,* text written by Gene Weingarten. This one-page essay falls well within our word limit for short writing, and yet the author changes the pace of the reading by alternating sentence length. With a pencil, mark up the text and analyze in the margins how he gets readers to move, and how he gets them to slow down or stop.

Stanley, 16

This is a breathtaking tale of yearning and desire, of daring and adventure, of the triumph of will. We're going to tell it in two hundred words. Warning: It's R-rated.

When Stanley the Jack Russell terrier was young and handsome, he was chosen to sire a litter. Alas, Stanley had the enthusiasm but not the height to properly woo the lovely but comparatively statuesque Hayley. No coupling occurred.

And so was arranged a different sort of conjugal event, at a veterinarian's office. There, in Hayley's presence but without her cooperation, through the practiced hand of a medical professional, Stanley was induced to surrender that which was needed.

The following evening when Debbie returned from work, Stanley was nowhere to be found. On her answering machine was a message from the vet: Stanley was on the front doorstep, wagging his tail hopefully. He had somehow escaped a fenced-in yard and run two miles through busy streets.

These days, in his senescence, Stanley sometimes gets a little foggy about where he is and where he is going. He can get lost. But he'll never lose the nickname he's carried ever since his Grand Adventure:

Manly Stanley.

Now, read the text again and this time mark the following:

- Any sentence that is no longer than five words
- The number of words in the sentences at the ends of paragraphs
- How these compare in length to the opening sentences in each paragraph
- The longest sentence
- The shortest sentence

Consider how these measurements inform your analysis of the pace of this story.

13

⚡

Hit your target.

A streamlined version of the change-of-pace trick is the *target* move. Imagine writing a long passage that looks like the flight of an arrow from a strong bow across a distance and into the center of a target. The bow is the *subject,* the bowstring is the *verb,* and the arrow crosses the distance of the message but stops suddenly on some emphatic point. The more humorous or satirical the passage, the sharper the point:

- "Groundhog Day has been observed only once in Los Angeles because when the groundhog came out of its hole, it was killed by a mud slide." (Johnny Carson)
- "When I was a boy, the Dead Sea was only sick." (George Burns)
- "When they circumcised Herbert Samuel, they threw away the wrong bit." (David Lloyd George on a rival)

Stephen Greenblatt is an author, a Harvard professor, and one of America's most public scholars. He has written award-winning books on Shakespeare's life and works and an oddly beautiful book on the influence of an ancient poem in the making of the modern world. The book is called *Swerve,* and in this passage on the philosophy of the Roman poet Lucretius, the author aims at and hits his target:

> That Lucretius and many others did more than simply associate themselves with Epicurus—that they celebrated him as godlike in his wisdom and courage—depended not on his social credentials but upon what they took to be the saving power of his vision. The core of this vision may be traced back to a single incandescent idea: that everything that has ever existed and everything that will ever exist is put together out of indestructible building blocks, irreducibly small in size, unimaginably vast in number. The Greeks had a word for these invisible building blocks, things that, as they conceived them, could not be divided any further: atoms.

If you are counting, there are 108 words in that paragraph. Who could doubt that the first 107 words are in service to the last one? Everything points to *atoms,* the word that will allow the arrow of the sentence to fly from a world of Roman aqueducts to one of quantum mechanics.

To demonstrate that this move is strategic rather than accidental, I can offer another example from Greenblatt, also from *Swerve.* In this passage, the author describes the special talent that turned a common worker named Poggio

Bracciolini (1380–1459) into one of the great book hunters and copiers of the Italian Renaissance:

> After the defeat of the *Ciompi,* as the working-class revolutionaries were called, the resurgent oligarchs held on to power tenaciously for more than forty years, shaping Poggio's whole knowledge and experience of the city where he determined to make his fortune. He had to find a way into a conservative, socially bounded world. Fortunately for him, by innate skill and training he possessed one of the few gifts that would enable someone of his modest origins and resources to do so. The key that opened the first door through which he slipped was something that has come to mean next to nothing in the modern world: beautiful handwriting.

Coincidentally, we have another paragraph of 108 words, and once again all the early words are in service of the last two. What follows any paragraph, of course, is a bar of white space that helps to show where the word marksman has hit his target dead center.

The target move turns out to be perfect for contemporary forms of short writing, as shown in these examples from *Twitter Wit:*

- "Some people don't like Vietnamese food, but I don't know what they're complaining pho." (@spdracerx)
- "I got an extra two years just because I laughed every time the judge said penal." (@Juniorwad)
- "You can't outsource balls." (@StephenAtHome)

As you continue your reading of short texts, new and old, keep these strategic moves in mind. You will begin to notice them more and more in your reading and can rehearse how to use them in your own writing.

GRACE NOTES

1. To practice hitting your target, try writing a short, focused paragraph, fiction or nonfiction, that ends with one of the following words or phrases:

> the world's greatest lover
> a chocolate stain
> moonwalk
> a one-armed man
> 007
> the greatest story never told
> Aunt Mabel's pajamas

2. Now make a list of words or phrases that have special meaning for you. Use them as targets, placing them at the end of paragraphs for special emphasis.

3. Because of its compression and emotional intensity, poetry often magnifies the effects of hitting the target. Read your favorite poets to check for this rhetorical move, as in this poem by Emily Dickinson:

> Surgeons must be very careful
> When they take the knife!
> Underneath their fine incisions
> Stirs the Culprit — *Life*!

14

~~~

Count to three.

Many topics, issues, or insights do not lend themselves to a "One, two, buckle my shoe" rendition. One-two may be perfect for comparison/contrast, creative tension, conflict, friction, frisson, the shock of recognition, or ironic juxtaposition. But there will be times when the writer hopes to capture the world beyond the limits of black and white, to frame the world in three dimensions, as a whole, as a microcosm, a complete unit of something larger. Enter the magic of *one-two-three*.

Let's begin with that ancient short form we call a prayer, in this case the famous Serenity Prayer composed by the theologian Reinhold Niebuhr:

> God grant me the serenity
> to accept the things I cannot change;

courage to change the things I can;
and the wisdom to know the difference.

Niebuhr wrote another stanza, but few can remember it because these first four lines say so much — in fact, they say it *all*, an illusion created by the magic of three. "God grant me," he writes, three things:

1. "Serenity to accept"
2. "Courage to change"
3. "Wisdom to know"

I argued in the book *Writing Tools* that if two examples divide the world, then the addition of a third element encompasses the world, creates at least the appearance of the whole, an effect made manifest in common discourse: beginning, middle, end; of the people, by the people, for the people; Moe, Larry, Curly; Tinker to Evers to Chance; faith, hope, love; truth, justice, and the American way; and many more.

Let's see how this pattern of three works in one of America's most famous short poems, "The Red Wheelbarrow," by William Carlos Williams:

so much depends
upon

a red wheel
barrow

glazed with rain
water

beside the white
chickens.

"Simplicity is the hallmark of William Carlos Williams's most original work," writes the critic Camille Paglia in *Break, Blow, Burn,* "which never loses its mysterious freshness.... Williams sought a common language to close the gap between poetry and everyday experience." She explains that "the poem is an extension of Imagism, a modernist Anglo-American movement influenced by unrhymed Asian poetry (such as haiku and tanka) that strictly limits the number of lines and syllables." In such poetry, "sharp physical details are presented but not explained: the images must speak for themselves."

The poet could have selected two or four details to compose his image, but he chooses three. We see (1) a red wheelbarrow, (2) the glaze of rainwater, (3) white chickens. The order is not random. Williams first asks us to stare at a work of human artifice, an object designed to enable the work of the farm. Although it is red, it bears an additional form of decoration, a reflective glaze—formed by a life-sustaining liquid—that coats the wheelbarrow as if it were a piece of pastry. The poet's final glance is toward living things, the white chickens, animals over which humans have claimed dominion, which produce meat, eggs, and money. So much depends upon these elements: life, wealth, domesticity, productive labor, community, and much more. I am not the first to notice that each stanza has the look of a small pictorial wheelbarrow. The key, though, is three.

The haiku, which has found a new life on Twitter, is a poetic form in which seventeen syllables are ordered into three lines. Here is a classic American haiku, written by the Beat author Jack Kerouac:

> In my medicine cabinet
> the winter fly
> has died of old age.

And another by Eric Amann (in the more standard five-seven-five syllable arrangement):

> Winter burial:
> a stone angel points his hand
> at the empty sky

What impresses me most in haiku is not a one-two tension, but a pattern of three, in which the first line marks place and/or time; the second introduces an object and an action; and the third opens a rich possibility of meanings.

Here @passepartout gives it a try for Twitter, well within the limit of 140 characters:

> Spring, my hair was gold
> Then waves of auburn followed
> It is pewter now

@uncjonny introduces modern techno-imagery:

> Was born analog
> Only to toil a lifetime
> To die digital

R. H. Blyth describes haiku as "an open door that looks shut," a definition that might apply to all the best forms of short writing. At a glance, the writing may be brief and clear on its surface. But linger, even for a moment, and the language begins to stretch itself out, inviting readers to do the same.

A similar pattern of three is visible in the spiritual ruminations of Dag Hammarskjöld, an influential secretary-general of the United Nations, whose diary was published under the title *Markings*. His first entry of 1953:

> "—Night is drawing nigh—"
> For all that has been—Thanks!
> To all that shall be—Yes!

In this next example, the three parts run on rather than stack up in poetic lines: "Goodness is something so simple: always to live for others, never to seek one's own advantage." Hammarskjöld offers readers something more complex in this next example, a pattern of three that looks like decorative serpents entwined on ancient gold jewelry:

> A line, a shade, a color—their fiery expressiveness.
> The language of flowers, mountains, shores, human bodies: the interplay of light and shade in a look, the ach-

ing beauty of a neckline, the grail of the white crocus on the alpine meadow in the morning sunshine—words in a transcendental language of the senses.

The first three nouns (*line, shade, color*) are itemized but then coalesced for what they have in common—their fire. We get a less obvious pattern of three in the interplay of light, the aching beauty of a neckline, and the grail of the white crocus, which once again are coalesced in their transcendental power. Three, which become one. The Trinity. Or as in Saint Paul's designation of the three great virtues: faith, hope, love, the greatest of which is one single virtue, love.

GRACE NOTES

1. Begin to notice in your reading the difference between patterns of two and patterns of three. Remember that two elements divide the world, inviting you to compare and contrast them. Three elements encompass the world, offering a sense of the whole.

2. Even if you have not written poetry before, try your hand at haiku. Use the traditional form: a line of five syllables, a line of seven syllables, and another of five syllables. Five, seven, five—a total of seventeen syllables in all. Traditional Japanese haiku focus on moments in nature: a flower down to its last petal, or a white flower reflecting the moonlight. Do a little haiku reporting—that is, closely observe a scene or moment in the natural world, gather key details, then write your poem.

3. Based on its effect on readers, the number three is the largest number in literature. Go on a literary scavenger hunt,

looking for examples from favorite writers (and your own work) of the versatility of three: three details, three examples, three names, three reasons, three acts in a play. From the sentence level to the structural level, you will find the power of three. Beginning, middle, and end.

15

<img / >

Inject the juice of parallels.

In studying thousands of examples of short writing, old and new, I've been amazed at how many of the most memorable depend on parallelism (with variation) to work their magic. The British playwright Tom Stoppard argued, "It's better to be quotable than to be honest." The balance here rests on the difference between "to be quotable" and "to be honest," equal grammatical units that describe equivalent ideas.

Consider this rich and varied sample, selected from an anthology compiled by Robert Byrne:

- "Show me a hero and I will write you a tragedy." (F. Scott Fitzgerald)
- "The higher the buildings, the lower the morals." (Noel Coward)

- "Drunkenness is the ruin of reason. It is premature old age. It is temporary death." (Saint Basil)
- "The poor wish to be rich, the rich wish to be happy, the single wish to be married, and the married wish to be dead." (Ann Landers)
- "You don't stop laughing because you grow old; you grow old because you stop laughing." (Michael Pritchard)

It should come as no surprise that the most quotable figures in literary culture are masters of parallelism. These examples appear in the work of the epigrammatic Oscar Wilde:

- "Twenty years of romance make a woman look like a ruin; but twenty years of marriage make her something like a public building." (*A Woman of No Importance*)
- "Find expression for a sorrow; and it will become dear to you. Find expression for a joy, and you intensify its ecstasy." ("The Critic as Artist")
- "Romance is the privilege of the rich, not the profession of the unemployed." ("The Model Millionaire")

In our own time, that kind of literary bite marked the work of the late Anglo-American author and critic Christopher Hitchens. Notice his parallel moves:

- "We are mammals and the prefrontal lobe (at least while we wait for genetic engineering) is too small while the adrenaline gland is too big." (*Letters to a Young Contrarian*)

- On Bill Clinton and Newt Gingrich, with the parallels expressed in a sequence of compound modifiers: "These two bloated, Southern-strategizing, God-bothering, pot-smoking, self-pitying, draft-dodging, wife-cheating, unreadable-book-writing, money-scrounging bigmouths and pseudo-intellectuals lean on each other like Pat and Mike, in a shame-free double-act where all the moves and gags are plotted in advance." (*Nation,* February 3, 1997)

James Geary's nifty history of the aphorism, *The World in a Phrase,* begins with this example from W. H. Auden on its cover: "Guessing is more fun than knowing," a bit of wisdom that seesaws from the weight of those two parallel gerunds. He cites examples juiced up with parallelism from writers as different as these:

- Baltasar Gracián: "First be master over yourself if you would be master over others."
- Benjamin Franklin: "Early to bed, and early to rise, makes a man healthy, wealthy, and wise."
- Ludwig Wittgenstein: "The limits of my language mean the limits of my world."

One of Geary's favorite definitions of the aphorism comes from Mark Twain, a master of the parallel construction: "A minimum of sound to a maximum of sense." Geary is also a fan of the double dose of parallelism known as the *chiasmus,* a word that derives from the Greek letter x (chi) and means a crossing: "In literary terms," writes Geary, "a chiasmus is a figure of speech in which the order of words in two parallel clauses is reversed. It is a popular aphoristic technique that often results in startling juxtapositions, such as Mae West's classic line: 'It's not the men in your life that matters, it's the life in your men.'"

Can we include "I'd rather have a bottle in front of me than a frontal lobotomy"? I now see the chi in "It's not the size of the dog in the fight that counts, but the size of the fight in the dog." Dare I suggest that when it comes to writing, it's not the length of the text that matters, but the power of the text for the length?

GRACE NOTES

1. Begin to notice in your reading parallel constructions wherever you encounter them. Write them in your daybook to get a sense of what they feel like as they flow from hand to page.

2. Review some pages of your writing, looking for opportunities to include parallels through revision. Remember that to create parallels, you need equal grammatical units to express equal ideas: "Shake, rattle, and roll."

3. Revise this sentence to make the key elements parallel: "He named his goldfish after female characters from Shakespeare: Juliet, Rosalind, Ophelia, the Queen of Egypt, Desdemona, and Caesar's wife."

16

~~~

Tweak the predictable.

I was enjoying breakfast with my friend and former boss Jim Naughton, a man known as the Merry Prankster of journalism for his legendary practical jokes, including his appearance at a presidential press conference wearing a costume chicken head. He was dressed less elaborately for breakfast, in jeans and a green T-shirt that read, "I avoid clichés like the plague."

OK, I get it, ha-ha, LOL, yada yada, funny bit, violating in the second part of the sentence the law established in the first. In an effort to top him—a dangerous thing to do with a man who once placed forty-six New Jersey bullfrogs in the executive restroom of a big-shot newspaper editor—I tweaked his chest billboard: "Wouldn't it be funnier if a dentist had written it?" I asked. "You know, I avoid clichés like the plaque."

For reasons I find hard to explain, we want great writing to be unpredictable and predictable at the same time — predictable in that the author creates a text, a story, a poem, that satisfies the reader by fulfilling a set of expectations, those expectations dictated by the genre (or story type) or by a tradition of storytelling. We expect Robin Hood to be a good rebel who "steals from the rich and gives to the poor," and we are willing to tolerate significant variations from scene to scene, but not an ending in which Robin joins up with the Sheriff of Nottingham to assassinate King Richard, then cheats on Maid Marian in an orgy with a six-pack of tavern wenches. Reader predictions work all the way down the ladder from the level of theme to the sentence level. So if I recited, "Robin Hood became beloved in England because he stole from the rich...," many folks familiar with the legend would be able to complete the sentence, "and gave to the poor."

But what if I wrote about a character named Robin who lived in the hood? What if I wrote that he stole from the rich and gave to his granny? Or he stole from the rich and gave to his 401(k)? Such variations might be disorienting at first for the reader, or a great source of surprise and delight.

If I read aloud the phrase "Once upon a...," most listeners would expect the predictable word "time." But if I were promoting the musical version of the fairy tale "The Princess and the Pea," I might surprise you with *Once upon a Mattress.*

This move — call it the *tweak* — has worked countless times, not just in supplying the surprise ending to a fully realized narrative, but also in making us laugh, think, and renew our love affair with the English language:

- "One more drink and I'd have been under the host" (Dorothy Parker). She tweaks the predictable phrase *under the table.*
- "Moderation is a fatal thing. Nothing succeeds like excess" (Oscar Wilde in *A Woman of No Importance*). Notice how this variation in the final word enhances the hit-the-target move. The author not only lands on the last word but transforms it.
- "God is love, but get it in writing" (Gypsy Rose Lee). In this case the famous burlesque queen takes a familiar religious phrase but does not end it in the predictable place, adding to faith a bit of mischievous skepticism.
- "Curiosity killed the cat, but for a while I was a suspect." (Steven Wright)
- "If at first you don't succeed, find out if the loser gets anything." (sports columnist Bill Lyon)

If we want to trace this rhetorical pattern in English literature, we would have to go back to the beginning, to Anglo-Saxon poetry (as in *Beowulf*), which worked off a four-beat poetic line in which the first three beats alliterated, but the final beat did not. Here's my original poem, designed to imitate the Old English style:

I live a life of language now
I read and write and rub the text

My fingers feel a fire there
Where hands and head and heart attend

It turns out to be a very congenial pattern for the eye and ear. The reader can see or hear the repetition that comes from alliteration (*hands, head, heart*), but is then relieved of what would become incessant thumping with a variation on the final note (*attend*). While the backbone of reading comes from predicting a pattern, the soul of it comes from brilliant surprise. Or, as Dorothy Parker explained, "Brevity is the soul of lingerie."

GRACE NOTES

In your daybook, or right on this page, transform the meaning of these common sayings by tweaking the final element in each, creating shock and delight. For example, "Early to bed, and early to rise, makes a man healthy, wealthy, and as boring as a pair of brown wing-tipped shoes."

1. A man's home is his castle.
2. Women's work is never done.
3. You show me yours, and I'll show you mine.
4. What we have here is a failure to communicate.
5. People in glass houses shouldn't throw stones.
6. If mama ain't happy, ain't nobody happy.
7. Youth is wasted on the young.
8. All you need is love. (How about "All you need is glove!" to describe a great defensive play by a major-league shortstop?)

17

~~~

Vary hard and soft words.

In January 1967, I began my first serious study of poetry under the tutelage of a brilliant young professor named Rene Fortin. The poetry was twentieth century, described as modern, and took us from William Carlos Williams to Sylvia Plath. The style of interpretation derived from a school called the New Criticism. Nothing mattered, I learned, except for the words on the page, especially any evidence of tension, ambivalence, or ambiguity.

The history of the period meant nothing. The poet's biography meant nothing. The author's intent, stated or hidden, meant nothing. I was told again and again to derive meaning from the complex dance of words on the page, especially in short, dense texts. Despite its several weaknesses as a way of interpreting literature, the New Criticism gave me the ability to read closely and with full attention. I would not be the same reader, writer, or teacher today without that skill.

I've been reading more poetry lately: Shakespeare's sonnets, twentieth-century anthologies, and now Emily Dickinson. This renewed study of poetry has helped me solve some problems in *How to Write Short* and has toned reading muscles that had gone a bit flabby. I am noticing things in old texts, for example, that I don't remember having seen in earlier readings. Consider two short poems written by the Belle of Amherst, Miss Emily Dickinson. Here is the first:

> A word is dead
> When it is said,
> Some say.
> I say it just
> Begins to live
> That day.

I would invite you to read the poem again, this time with attention to the length of the words. I count nineteen words in all. Each word, with the exception of *begins,* has one syllable. The total number of letters is fifty-nine. That means that the average length of a word equals 3.1 letters, astonishing efficiency by any measure.

Another poem:

> "Faith" is a fine invention
> When Gentlemen can *see*—
> But *Microscopes* are prudent
> In an Emergency.

Let's do the math. By one standard, this poem is shorter, containing only sixteen words. But wait! It runs to 77 letters, on the back of the polysyllabic words *invention, gentlemen, microscopes,* and *emergency.* The average word length is about 4.8 letters.

This "tale of the tape," as they say when measuring the physical attributes of boxers, reveals something essential about the nature of the English language. English is, at the same time, a hard language and a soft language. (Here's a different version of that last sentence: "English is, simultaneously, a hard language and a soft language.") Notice that English gives me two ways of saying the same thing: *at the same time* and *simultaneously,* four words adding up to thirteen letters, or one fourteen-letter word.

The hard stock of English words comes from our Anglo-Saxon heritage. In addition to function words such as prepositions and conjunctions, the Old English word hoard contained many stark words of one syllable, including the notorious four-letter variety. Notice how "hard" the language of Dickinson's first poem sounds and feels. It's all heavy jabs with the pop, pop, pop, pop sound of *word, dead, live,* and *day.*

That hard language was softened in 1066 after the invasion of England by William the Conqueror. The Norman (think French) king brought with him a language that sounded more sophisticated and urbane. Words derived from Latin and Greek, with migration routes through Italy and France, were suited to the workings of government and to higher levels of abstraction. Most of the key words in the second poem—*invention, gentlemen, microscopes, prudent, emergency*—have grown into English from Latin and French roots.

In her book *Break, Blow, Burn,* the critic Camille Paglia writes:

> What fascinated me about English was what I later recognized as its hybrid etymology: blunt Anglo-Saxon concreteness, sleek Norman French urbanity, and polysyllabic Greco-Roman abstraction. The clash of these elements, as competitive as Italian dialects, is invigorating, richly entertaining, and often funny, as it is to Shakespeare, who gets tremendous effects out of their interplay. The dazzling multiplicity of sounds and word choices in English makes it brilliantly suited to be a language of poetry.

But not just poetry.

Check out this passage from a favorite writer, M. F. K. Fisher, from her collection of essays *The Art of Eating* (it comes after a recipe for oyster loaf):

> For me at least, that recipe is at last the one I have been looking for. I can change it as I will, and even pour a little thick cream over the loaf, or dust it with cayenne, but basically it is right with my childhood dream...and quite probably it is much better than the one the young ladies ate in their stuffy lamp-lit rendezvous so many years ago.
>
> And yet...yet those will always be in my mental gastronomy, on my spiritual taste-buds, the most delicious oysters I never ate.

I love the way the hot, exotic word *cayenne* arrives after twenty of the twenty-one previous words tumble out in monosyllables, like marbles from a bag; the way that *stuffy lamp-lit* abuts with the romantic *rendezvous,* and *spiritual* with *taste-buds;* especially the way that *mental gastronomy* and *delicious oysters* hit a full stop with *I never ate.* This is a lady who cooks not just with the ingredients of food, but with the many flavors of the English language, combining the hearty native elements of her soup stock with the most elegant and subtle of Continental spices.

GRACE NOTES

1. Use the Anglo-Saxon word stock to create a staccato effect or to end a phrase with a snap or punch.

2. Make a random list of English synonyms in which one word in a pair is short and the other long. To get you started: *lit/illuminated; jail/incarcerate; piss/urinate.*

3. Look through your recent writing to see if you can substitute a long word for a short one, or vice versa. Which feels better to you?

4. Read the passages aloud to check for pace, rhythm, flow, style, and meaning.

18

Join the six-word discipline.

In the last few chapters, you have learned several writing moves that can be especially effective in short writing. You've learned to balance and unbalance your sentences and paragraphs; to change the pace in your writing; to hit your target. You've learned that two language or story elements divide the world for readers, but that three encompass that same world. Whether your structure is one-two or one-two-three, parallels can make your work more readable and memorable. You can even tweak the final elements to the surprise and delight of your readers. Part of the friction in short prose can come in the strategic selection of the "hard" and "soft" words and cadences in the English language.

To build those short writing muscles, practice these strategies in six words.

Inspired by a six-word story attributed to Hemingway,

"For sale: baby shoes, never worn," writers have joined a literary movement that might be called the six-word revolution. It's not clear whether Ernest "Old Papa Fuzzy-Face" Hemingway invented this bit of microfiction or merely plucked it out of a newspaper's classified ads section. Why were the shoes never worn? Most readers assume that the baby died. But what if he was born without feet? Or with feet so big that regular baby shoes would not fit her?

It's fun to play with the pattern:

"For sale: every politician in America."
"For sale: My remaindered books. Cheap."
"For sale: condoms, way too small."

While Hemingway, godfather of the terse style, may have sparked the six-word revolution, it was the online story site *Smith* that fanned the fire. Its editor, Larry Smith, invited readers — apprentices and masters — to submit six-word memoirs. The best of these were anthologized in *Not Quite What I Was Planning* (2008), whose title itself is an example of the form.

In a lively introduction, the editors of *Smith* emphasize the range of experiences (life, death, loss, hope, fear, joy) that can be described in six words. They also note the radical modulations of tone and style, from formal to familiar, from straight to ironic. I would encourage you to visit the *Smith* magazine website and Sixwordmemoirs.com and to taste as many of these ministories as you can stand. Then sit down for twenty minutes and write your own. To help you figure out your range of choices, I offer these examples, highlighting the strategies that created them.

Target

Among my favorite examples is the single simple sentence that ends with a supercharged word or phrase. In a sense the story is told in one word, a target, with the five earlier words performing an opening act.

"I grew up in a cemetery," written by Rachael Hanel, is a perfect example of this move. Notice how the sentence builds with one-syllable words. Then it hits us with the offbeat climax, a long word that takes up almost half the line.

It reminds me of a favorite line from Shakespeare, when a messenger informs Macbeth: "The Queen, my lord, is dead." It could have been, "The Queen is dead, my lord," but the Bard wants to give the full emphasis to *dead*.

Change of Pace

A variation on the previous move is the sentence without a verb, also known as the intentional fragment. The writer still shines a light on the final word but adds a little razzle-dazzle. Arthur Raz wrote, "Ringo was my favorite Beatle. Really."

David Temple created the same effect: "I won at Scrabble today. Word."

One-Two Punch

In this move the writer creates a balanced sentence, the second half taking something back from the first. Building on a parallel structure, Chris Cooper writes, "Was big boy, now little man." This one-two punch by Taylor Stump is a bit off center (two words, then four), which adds to the effect: "Canoe guide, only got lost once."

One-Two-Three

Two elements in a sentence divide the load, but three create a more rounded feeling, communicating to the reader a sense of the whole: beginning, middle, end. Check out this editorial by Rabih Alameddine: "American backbone, Arab marrow, much trouble." Here's a three-step take on ethnicity by Jeannie Lee: "Asian, white trash Scranton. Let's Polka."

Inventory

Let's add to our short writing toolbox the inventory or list. Include enough elements—as with the more than fifty-eight thousand names of the dead on the Vietnam Veterans Memorial—and short becomes a readable long text. But a list can be a list with only six words. Josh Rosenfield offered his critique of mediated reality: "Adolescence, internet, internet, internet, internet, death." Colleen Zachary used rhyme to connect the private parts, so to speak: "Affection. Erection. No protection. Injection. Infection." Maybe a little Rejection or Inspection would have led to some Detection.

There are more uses to a well-crafted six-word text than we've seen so far. One is the act of literary distillation, the ability to describe the most powerful theme or premise of a story in six words or less. Here are some examples I've drawn from popular television programs:

"Blond California teen undemons the world." (*Buffy the Vampire Slayer*)
"Waste management business: corpses in Jersey." (*The Sopranos*)
"Cuban bandleader marries ditzy redheaded housewife." (*I Love Lucy*)
"Philly teens boppin', hoppin', on TV." (*American Bandstand*)
"Masked man, Indian friend, silver bullets." (*The Lone Ranger*)

Or try using six words not just to distill action but to capture the essential message of a text:

"Man cannot live by revenge alone." (*Moby-Dick*)
"Children offer more wisdom than adults." (*The Catcher in the Rye*)
"Racism is not inborn. It's learned." (*Huckleberry Finn*)
"The rich are not like us." (*The Great Gatsby*)
"True love is expressed through sacrifice." ("The Gift of the Magi")

Remember your goal: to become a master of the short form. You can tone your muscles with exercise that includes the three behaviors that define all literate people: read short, write short, and talk about the craft of reading and writing short. Now try it in six words. (He said, using just six words.) (Again.)

GRACE NOTES

Give yourself five minutes to write five six-word phrases using each of the moves described above. Ready, steady, go! Here are mine:

- *Target word:* "Funniest word I know is zipper."
- *Change of pace:* "Dyslexic Mel Brooks in frustration: 'Yo.'"
- *One-two punch:* "Playing a hunch, married in Vegas."
- *One-two-three:* "New typewriters, old reporters, worn out."
- *Inventory:* "Decapitation, defenestration, deforestation, desalination, detention, determination."

OK, so it took me fifteen minutes to crank these out. But such play and practice will help you develop the basic moves that will lead to more sophisticated improvisations.

19

Cut it short.

I am ready to rebel against one of the most revered statements ever uttered by a teacher of writing. Delivered to his Cornell students over decades, this phrase was written by Professor William Strunk Jr. in the original version of *The Elements of Style:* "Omit needless words." To which he added a now oft-quoted paragraph:

> Vigorous writing is concise. A sentence should contain no unnecessary words, a paragraph no unnecessary sentences, for the same reason that a drawing should have no unnecessary lines and a machine no unnecessary parts. This requires not that the writer make all his sentences short, or that he avoid all detail and treat his subjects only in outline, but that he make every word tell.

I count sixty-five words in this worthy or wordy paragraph. So which is it? Worthy or wordy? To answer that question, I decided to try reining in that paragraph within the corral of a 140-character tweet. Such an experiment might reveal pathways to intelligent cutting. I began by plugging the paragraph into Twitter to find that those sixty-five words equaled 386 characters, 246 over the limit. I looked for ways to whittle it down:

> Vigorous writing is concise. A sentence should contain no extra words for the same reason that a drawing should have no extra lines. Not all sentences need be short and without detail. But every word must tell.

What have we done here?

- Preserved the topic sentence
- Substituted the shorter *extra* for *unnecessary* (not exact synonyms, but close)
- Cut the analogy to a machine, preserving the one about drawing, which is more organic and protects the use of *lines,* a measurement for both artists and writers
- Kept the focus on the writing and not the writer, eliminating words necessary to describe the producer in favor of the product

That got us from sixty-five to thirty-seven words, bringing the character count from 386 to 211, much tighter, but still not within Twitter margins. Let's try again:

Strong writing is concise. A text should have no extra words like a drawing with no extra lines. A sentence can be long with detail. But every word must tell.

We've cut seven words and are down to 159 characters. Where will I find more "needless" words? I gained space by turning *vigorous* to *strong* and *sentence* to *text,* but I feel a slide toward brevity at the loss of nuance. But let's not stop now:

Strong prose is tight. A text needs no extra words like a drawing with no extra lines. A phrase can be long with detail. But every word must tell.

One hundred forty-six characters. Almost there:

Write tight. A text needs no extra words as a drawing needs no extra lines. A sentence can be long with detail. But every word must tell.

One hundred thirty-seven characters. Bingo! Three to spare. But at what cost?

Even E. B. White saw the problem and described it in his introduction to the book that would become known as Strunk and White:

"Omit needless words!" cries the author on page 17, and into that imperative Will Strunk really put his heart and soul. In the days when I was sitting in his class, he omitted so many needless words, and omitted them so forcibly and with such eagerness and obvious relish, that he often seemed in the position of having short-changed himself, a man left with nothing more to say yet with time to fill, a radio prophet who had outdistanced the clock. Will Strunk got out of this predicament by a simple trick: he uttered every sentence three times. When he delivered his oration on brevity to the class, he leaned forward over his desk, grasped his coat lapels in his hands, and in a husky, conspiratorial voice said, "Rule Thirteen. Omit needless words! Omit needless words! Omit needless words!"

Too bad, because there's more to say about that famous phrase, especially if each word is placed under scrutiny: *omit, needless, words.* (By the way, Mr. White, I wonder what Professor Strunk might have said about your phrase "grasped his coat lapels in his hands." Did you need *coat*? Where else would he find lapels? And did you need *in his hands*? What else would he grasp them with?)

Merriam-Webster's defines *omit* as "to leave out or leave unmentioned." The literal and connotative meanings of the word lean toward the negative. There is the sense that something has been left out that could or should have been expressed. Compared to a sin of commission (as in Sir Arthur Quiller-Couch's "Murder your darlings"), there is something soft, tentative, if not sheepish, in Strunk's injunction that needless words should not even be "committed" to the page for examination.

My discomfort may come from that distinction among writers between the putter-inners and the taker-outers.

While most writers will on occasion go both ways, these differences are real. The first group will write a draft teeming with information, scenes, evidence, references, cases—whatever helps to make a story more compelling or an argument more solid. We put in whatever might be relevant. During revision, we take out the stuff that does not fit our focus. The second group, the taker-outers, will edit—mentally or physically—while they draft, making decisions as soon as they can about the removal of elements they find unnecessary. A putter-inner writes a tweet of 260 characters and cuts back to 140. A taker-outer may offer only 100 characters in a first take, adding 40 more if necessary.

While I'll never be mentioned in the same breath as Thomas Wolfe, who delivered manuscripts to Scribner's Maxwell Perkins in moving vans, I did send to Tracy Behar at Little, Brown a manuscript for *The Glamour of Grammar* that was twice the agreed-on length. I put in everything I could think of in an almost manic race to deadline. Tracy guided me diplomatically through the effort to take out 65,000 words, or fifty extra chapters, enough stuff for another book, however substandard.

So if your assignment is to write 300 words, are you better off writing 250 and then filling out to the margins by revision? Or 350 and then deleting the least helpful words? There is no right answer, except for this: A good short writer must be a disciplined cutter, not just of clutter, but of language that would be useful if she had more space. How, what, and when to cut in the interest of brevity, focus, and precision must preoccupy the mind of every good short writer.

Which brings us back to Strunk's *needless*. To use such a

word is like saying that lawyers should charge a "fair" price for their services. While most would favor the idea, the fighting would be fervent over the meaning of *fair*—and the meaning of *needless*. Each reader will bring a different level of need to the act of reading, so the writer is likely to make decisions on word choice based on some crude utilitarian notion of the greatest good for the greatest number. What if I chose to delete the Strunk sentence "Vigorous writing is concise" and to begin with the idea, "A sentence should contain no unnecessary words"? We'd have to vote to determine who among us found Strunk's sentence on vigor and concision needed or needless.

Here's how I think *needless* works as a piece of advice for writers. Writers should scrutinize each word through drafting and revision. "Do I really need you?" is the question that will apply standards and help writers make good choices about what to include.

Finally, *words*, though simple and straightforward, may not be as helpful as the word seems on first blush. "Omit needless words" suggests that the writer should begin to cut a text at the word level. I am on the prowl for big things to take out. Omitting or cutting words is nickeling-and-diming a text. I want to cut big pieces if I can—twenty-dollar bills, not dimes and nickels. Remember Donald Murray's aphorism: "Brevity comes from selection and not compression." I begin, as I wrote in *Writing Tools,* by pruning the big limbs before I shake out the dead leaves.

To find and trim weaker elements in our prose (those dead leaves), identify and preserve the stronger elements. In the Anglo-American tradition, strength manifests itself in specific, concrete nouns (especially in the subject position) followed by vigorous, active transitive verbs. Concrete nouns give the reader things they can see (*mosquito, potato chip, clothespin, vise* rather than *vice*). Active verbs reveal the action performed by the subject (*blasted, yawned, gurgled, sprung*). Transitive verbs require an object. The full effect is a clear and direct sense of who did what: "The whiskey blurred his vision." When such elements are deemed strong, the weaker elements reveal themselves as targets for cutting.

Here is a list of the usual suspects:

- Adverbs
- Adjectives
- Strings of prepositional phrases (used as adjectives or adverbs)
- Intensifiers (*very, quite, incredibly*)
- Qualifiers (*seems, kind of, sort of, mostly*)
- Jargon (*instructional units* rather than *lessons*)
- Latinate flab (*adjudicate* rather than *judge*)

Most authors I know cut weak words as they find them, but some have organized their cutting strategies into useful categories. In his book *Style,* for example, Joseph M. Williams offers his "Five Principles of Concision":

1. Delete words that mean little or nothing [*kind of, really, actually*].
2. Delete words that repeat the meaning of other words [*various and sundry*].
3. Delete words implied by other words [*terrible tragedy*].

4. Replace a phrase with a word [*in the event that* becomes *if*].

5. Change negatives to affirmatives [*not include* becomes *omit*].

In *The Writer's Chapbook,* the editor George Plimpton reveals that no matter how famous the writer, the challenge remains the same: what to include and what to cut. Among his witnesses:

- Charles Dickens: "Run a moist pen slick through everything, and start afresh."
- Samuel Johnson: "Read over your compositions, and where ever you meet a passage which you think is particularly fine, strike it out."
- Ben Jonson: "The players have often mentioned it as an honor to Shakespeare, that in his writing, whatsoever he penned, he never blotted out a line. My answer hath been, 'Would he had blotted a thousand.'" (There is now good evidence that Shakespeare did!)

And what writer cannot identify with Oscar Wilde's indecision: "This morning I took out a comma and this afternoon I put it back in again."

GRACE NOTES

1. Write a brief description of your writing process, identifying yourself as a putter-inner or a taker-outer, or as someone in between.

2. Review E. B. White's description of his professor William Strunk Jr. Following my lead, look for words in the passage that White's teacher might have found "needless."

3. Review my multiple revisions of Strunk's paragraph, designed to cut it to the length of a tweet. At which revision do you feel something important is lost? At what point does the voice no longer sound like Strunk's?

4. Remember Donald Murray's advice, "Brevity comes from selection and not compression." And mine: "First prune the big limbs, then shake out the dead leaves."

5. Apply the "Five Principles of Concision" to a recent example of your writing. Record in your daybook the words and phrases you were able to cut.

20

Add by contraction.

I have often described the language of digital media as being contractive, elliptical, acronymic, and emoticonic—the kind of text squeezed onto a personalized license plate. At its best, such language is quick, informal, and effective. At times, though, it violates a practical principle that marks communication in all cultures: redundancy. Writing stylists attack redundancy as needless repetition. The information scholar James Gleick has a different take:

> Redundancy—inefficient by definition—serves as the antidote to confusion. It provides second chances. Every natural language has redundancy built in; this is why people can understand text riddled with errors and why they can understand conversation in a noisy room. The natural redundancy of English motivates the famous

New York City subway poster of the 1970s (and the poem by James Merrill),

> if u cn rd ths
> u cn gt a gd jb w hi pa!

After I wrote a column about my disinclination to use common text slang and abbreviations, I got a big thumbs-down from none other than the famed movie critic Roger Ebert, who twitted (I mean tweeted): "WTF? I'm to [*sic*] *old* 2 use 'LOL?' ROFL @ these ageist SOBs." Someone rushed to my defense: "@ebertchicago: You can pull off whatever language works for you & your audience: @roypeterclark was saying he couldn't pull off LOL." Can you imagine Ward Cleaver saying to the Beaver: "Slip me some skin, daddy-o"? Each of us seeks the level of language (including text slang, abbreviations, and contractions) that best serves our writing purposes, our authentic voices, and the most urgent needs of our audiences.

I notice that some writers of my generation (baby boomers) find opportunities to play with text slang in satirical ways, perhaps to mask their fear of being totally out of it. Gene Weingarten wondered what would have happened if Lincoln had decided to tweet the Gettysburg Address: "87 years ago, our dads made us free. Yay! Still want free, but hard! Fighting, dying, burying! Need more fight tho, so dead be happy."

In the *New Yorker,* William Sorensen even suggests some text slang that would work best for the geezer crowd:

- "NSR = Need some roughage"
- "JDTV? = Which channel has a Judi Dench movie tonight?"
- "RxV → BW = Got Viagra prescription, just need Barry White cassettes"

Ashley Parker, a young reporter at the *New York Times,* took some heat from her friends when she began using slang abbreviations favored by her teenage sister's crowd. In that world, influenced no doubt by incessant texting, the language, better known as "the ling," contracts to the squeezing point. *Definitely* became *def. Whatever* became *whatev. Obviously* became *obvi. Awkward* became *awk. Hilarious* became *hilar.*

But let's turn from text and teen slang to more traditional forms of language contraction. The *American Heritage Dictionary*'s definition of *contraction* contains helpful examples: "A word, as *won't* from *will not,* or phrase, as *o'clock* from *of the clock,* formed by omitting or combining some of the sounds of a longer phrase."

Let's (a contraction) do the math: Turning *will not* into *won't* saves three letters or, if you are on Twitter, three characters (including the space). So it's easy to see how contractions save space, especially when they involve function words rather than the most distinctive language. But contractions come with a side effect.

The more contractions used in a text, the less formal it will read and sound—often, but not always, a desirable effect. In his book *Legal Writing in Plain English,* Bryan A. Garner writes:

The relaxed tone, achieved partly through contractions, shows confidence.

The point about contractions isn't to use them whenever possible, but rather whenever natural. Like pronouns, they make a document more readable.

He then quotes that champion of plain English, Rudolf Flesch: "*Write as You Talk* is the accepted rule of writing readably—and in English, the most conspicuous and handiest device of doing that is to use contractions."

If you are writing a formal letter or document, especially if it's short, avoid contractions and most other abbreviations as well. Formal language spells things out, even dates and numbers. It takes no shortcuts at the word level. We all understand levels of formality as they apply to the writing of letters, e-mails, and other messages. The author of this Western Union telegram, dated January 22, 1945, avoids contractions in an effort to establish the most dignified tone within the confines of the form, as befits the solemn occasion of the message:

THE SECRETARY OF WAR DESIRES ME TO EXPRESS HIS DEEP REGRET THAT YOUR SON PRIVATE [JOHN JONES] WAS KILLED IN ACTION ON THREE JANUARY IN BELGIUM. CONFIRMING LETTER FOLLOWS.

[signed] ADJUTANT GENERAL

Imagine the lack of decorum that would have resulted if the author of that telegram had taken shortcuts, perhaps by using "Sctry" of War, or rendering the date "Jan. 3."

Most telegrams, of course, were written for much more mundane occasions. With costs by the word, abbreviated forms of communication resulted in less formality and occasional humor, as when a Hollywood reporter wanted to check out the age of a famous actor: HOW OLD CARY GRANT? To which the actor replied, OLD CARY GRANT FINE. HOW YOU?

GRACE NOTES

1. Master text slang and other forms of contraction and abbreviation before they master you.

2. Just because you've learned the shorthand style of digital communication doesn't mean that it should become your standard. Tune your voice to best fulfill your purpose and serve your audience.

3. Think of contractions—or the lack of them—as rhetorical tools. Here is the grammarian Martha Kolln, author of *Rhetorical Grammar:* "It's important to recognize the connection between the level of formality and the use of contractions: In general, the more formal the writing, the fewer contractions you'll find, or want to use, especially contracted auxiliaries [*John'll* for *John will*]. However, in most of the writing you do for school or on the job, the occasional contraction will certainly be appropriate. It's important to recognize the contribution that contractions can make to your personal voice." (Notice that Kolln uses three contractions to help familiarize her voice and soften the diction in an academic text.)

21

Excerpt — but in context.

I was in Atlanta when I learned of a controversy over an inscription marking the new Dr. Martin Luther King Jr. Memorial in Washington, DC. The quote on one side of the granite Stone of Hope reads, "I was a drum major for justice, peace and righteousness."

In an interview with the *Washington Post,* the poet Maya Angelou argued that these were not King's exact words and that, out of context, they made a humble preacher look like "an arrogant twit." It was not enough for Angelou that fourteen other quotations from Dr. King appear on a 450-foot memorial wall behind his statue.

By coincidence, this news ran as I began research for this book. I had already learned that we often use the shortest texts to express the most important messages, especially to honor and enshrine, and that we commonly use short excerpts from longer works to accomplish the task.

But too much concision can result in a loss of context.

I visited the monument to see for myself. The over-whelming impression of the new memorial derives not from language, but from sculpture. Even small photos of the new statue make Dr. King look monumental. He stands thirty feet tall, strong and determined, arms folded, looking as if he has just marched out of the huge block of stone behind him.

As impressive as the King monument appears, the drum-major inscription sounded to some a bit off-key. I thought I knew most of King's famous sayings, but this one was new to me. While it seemed wise not to fall back on the too familiar "I Have a Dream" speech, the marching-band metaphor felt uncharacteristic of King's usual rhetorical posture.

It turns out that Angelou's concerns were echoed by other African American scholars and leaders, who argued that the ten words on the monument base had been ripped from their original context and meaning. In a sermon deliv-ered at Atlanta's Ebenezer Baptist Church, just months before his death in 1968, King had preached, "Yes, if you want to say that I was a drum major, say that I was a drum major for justice. Say that I was a drum major for peace. I was a drum major for righteousness. And all of the other shallow things will not matter."

In context, the word *if* makes all the difference. Without that opening conditional clause, it does seem that Dr. King is embracing the role of drum major rather than acquiescing to it. This is not to say that Dr. King was always self-effacing. In a clairvoyant final speech before his assassination, King compares himself to Moses, the flawed prophet who led his people out of slavery, who had been to the mountaintop, who had seen the Promised Land, but who would not live long enough to get there with his people.

At the Poynter Institute we have created a central garden where students can relax and study. The path is lined with marble plaques, each containing an inspirational quotation. The famous writing teacher Donald Murray quotes from the Roman poet Horace: "Nulla dies sine linea," Latin for "Never a day without a line" (of writing). The engraver, not schooled in Latin, left out the word *sine* (without), leaving us with dead-language gibberish that could be taken to mean the opposite of the original.

"Oh, well," I said when I saw the mistake, "at least it's not carved in stone."

Everything I've learned about the language of enshrinement suggests that the inscription on the King monument should be revised. It need not be changed right away or in a way that would embarrass those who chose the original. Any revision should grow from a desire to perfect for posterity a magisterial work that springs from the noblest intentions.

I know of no written standards for historical inscriptions, but the unwritten ones could come down to these two: (1) quotations from the dead should never be taken out of context; and (2) quotations should reveal the honored character in the proper light—or a better light. The drum-major inscription fulfills neither of these standards.

To restore most of the original context would require the addition of twelve short words: "If you want to say that I was a drum major, say that..." A tighter compromise could be, "If you say I was a drum major, say..." At the very least, a single word added to the existing quotation would restore a bit of Dr. King's intended meaning: "Say I was a drum major for peace..."

Every writer I know has had an editor who, to save space, has cut a passage to the bone. When it's done well, the meaning can ring clearer with fewer words. When it's done poorly, something critical to the reader's understanding is left behind. The problem is serious enough when it occurs on paper or in pixels, even more serious when it's carved in stone.

There are special moments when voices are heard, when smart and caring people pause to think, when even governments are moved to do the right thing. A subsequent column by Rachel Manteuffel in the *Washington Post* cited arguments that persuaded the Department of the Interior to revise the King quote on the national memorial and restore its full and proper context. She quotes Maya Angelou, members of the King family, and an earlier version of this chapter published on CNN.com. The lesson: Getting it right is important. Revision can work at any stage of the process, even after a story has been published, even after a monument has been erected.

GRACE NOTES

1. The excerpt is a powerful form of short writing. Select the best or most relevant materials from others as evidence for your own arguments and essays.

2. Even if you are using an excerpt in a new context, make sure that it does not violate the spirit of the original work. Much harm is done by ripping someone's words out of their original context. Embrace responsible practice by checking an excerpt for accuracy and context.

3. When you cut a longer quotation down to size, be sure to use punctuation—such as quotation marks and ellipses—to signal that something has been left out.

22

〰️

Surprise with brevity.

In the fourth grade I memorized and delivered the Gettysburg Address to my parochial school classmates. I can't remember the assignment that inspired my performance, but I do recall that I was more parrot than poet, reciting Lincoln by rote with no understanding of historical context or of the meaning of individual words and phrases, beginning with "Four score and seven..." The only "four score" I knew was a grand-slam home run at Yankee Stadium.

Still, I grade that now-distant experience as among the most formative of my life. It put my young brain to hard work. It put me in front of an audience. And it put on my lips what is arguably the greatest short piece of writing in American history.

Five versions of the speech survive, along with news accounts from the period. The standard version is 269 words, and experts believe it contains revisions that Abraham Lincoln made himself so that his best thoughts could be preserved for posterity in the best language.

As a schoolboy, I was told that the president had scribbled the speech on the back of an envelope during the train ride from Washington to Pennsylvania battle sites. The tale turns out not to be true, but I embraced it as a kid. If little George Washington could chop down a cherry tree and then own up to it, surely Honest Abe could push a pen on the back of an envelope.

Such civic parables may mask a more inspiring history. Lincoln looked terrible that day and complained of illness, and some scholars speculate that he may have been suffering from a form of smallpox. The president was not the main speaker at the cemetery dedication and—already ill and fatigued—had to endure a stem-winder of more than two hours by former senator and Harvard College president Edward Everett, considered the most celebrated orator of his day.

Hostile editorialists criticized Lincoln's address as short, shallow, and unworthy of the civic liturgy. But for most who heard or read it, the speech became famous *because* of its brevity. Let's do the math. Everett spoke for two hours; Lincoln for two minutes. The now-forgotten oration was sixty times longer than the Gettysburg Address.

To Everett's credit, no one recognized the disparity or gave Lincoln more props than he did. "I should be glad," wrote Everett in a letter to his president, "if I could flatter myself that I came as near to the central idea of the occasion, in two hours, as you did in two minutes."

The obvious difference in the two speeches was length,

but that was not the only difference. Though there is a formality to Lincoln's language that to modern eyes seems appropriate for the occasion, in the shadow of Everett's classical oration, the president's speech seems as spare as a Quaker meeting room. Here is a quick sample of Everett's speech—and remember, as you read it, that back then long dramatic orations were considered forms of public entertainment:

> It was appointed by law in Athens, that the obsequies of the citizens who fell in battle should be performed at the public expense, and in the most honorable manner. Their bones were carefully gathered up from the funeral pyre, where their bodies were consumed, and brought home to the city. There, for three days before the interment, they lay in state, beneath tents of honor, to receive the votive offerings of friends and relatives,—flowers, weapons, precious ornaments, painted vases, (wonders of art, which after two thousand years adorn the museums of modern Europe,)—the last tributes of surviving affection.

Imagine having to sit or stand through two hours of this, waiting for President Lincoln's two minutes. As I read the speech, it does not surprise me that as Harvard's president, Everett was unpopular with the students, who referred to him as Granny.

In his book *Lincoln at Gettysburg,* historian Garry Wills asserts that the famous speech helped create a new form of political discourse, "a revolution in style." Sonorous and bombastic language gave way to the plain and simple—with this caveat:

It would be wrong to think that Lincoln moved toward the plain style of the Gettysburg just by writing shorter, simpler sentences. Actually, that Address ends with a very long sentence — eighty-two words, almost a third of the whole talk's length.

Wills argues that at their best "Lincoln's words acquired a flexibility of structure, a rhythmic pacing, a variation in length of words and phrases and clauses and sentences, that make his sentences move 'naturally,' for all their density and scope."

Not only could Lincoln draft great short writing, but he could find it in the unpolished work of others. The most persuasive example of the president's "verbal workshop" comes from a revision of his adviser William Seward. For the conclusion to the First Inaugural Address, Seward had suggested:

> The mystic chords which, proceeding from so many battlefields and so many patriot graves, pass through all the hearts and all the hearths in this broad continent of ours, will yet harmonize in their ancient music when breathed upon by the guardian angels of the nation.

Lincoln takes the frothy sentence and applies the tools of an old-timey newspaper rewrite-man:

> The mystic chords of memory, stretching from every battlefield and patriot grave, to every living heart and hearthstone, all over this broad land, will yet swell the chorus of the Union, when again touched, as surely they will be, by the better angels of our nature.

New Yorker editor Dorothy Wickenden describes the effect this way: "Lincoln took the sentiment, stripped it of its orotundity, and produced one of the most stirring political statements in American history." The lesson for those who write short is that brevity loves company—in the form of substance and style.

This book began with the reflection that the right words in the right order might be worth a thousand pictures. When I hear the famous words of Lincoln, or a recitation of the Twenty-Third Psalm, or the final, climactic litany of Dr. King standing before the crowds at the Lincoln Memorial, I close my eyes and hear and then see images, word pictures that fill my heart and fire up my soul, language that sets my imagination soaring.

There is a lesson here for all of us. Students, teachers, workers, bosses—most citizens find themselves with the duty of having to deliver a report, a presentation, a case study, a sermon, a speech. We know that this task—while common and important—often induces great anxiety in the speaker. One way to accomplish the task with the minimum amount of performance anxiety is to remember Honest Abe and keep the message short. Think of how grateful you are as a listener when the graduation speaker, no matter how powerful, delivers the goods in ten minutes rather than twenty, or, even better, five minutes rather than ten.

GRACE NOTES

1. Work from a ritual of reduction. Apply a 75 percent rule; that is, deliver the work in three-quarters of the

expected length. To get to that length, apply the strategies of cutting described earlier in this book, giving special attention to writing, and then speaking, with a sharp focus.

2. If you are afraid that the 75 percent rule will make your work look somehow deficient, you can extend the work to 90 percent. Even that will set you apart from the typical presenter, who promises, "I don't want this to be a lecture. I want it to be a conversation. So I've left lots of time for your questions and comments." What happens, of course, is seemingly endless presentation with a final shuffling of papers to try to fit everything in. By maintaining the spirit of Lincoln's address, you will create time for the audience to digest your thoughts and to share their own.

3. Rehearse your report or story for length. Don't just guess how long it will take to read. Time your reading, then make decisions about content and audience.

II

How to Write Short with a Purpose

When you learn short, the most important purposes of short writing soon become apparent. When I write short, it is to honor and enshrine, to crack wise and actually sound wise, to summarize and define, to sell and persuade, to report in real time and narrate, to link and think, and, probably most of all, to get attention.

People who know me will roll their eyes when they see that last aim. In a memorable piece of short writing, my mother, Shirley Clark, recorded in a baby book that I was the talk of the mothers on the Lower East Side of Manhattan: "Roy enjoys talking all the time, and attracts lots of attention by singing songs to anyone who will listen." Sheesh. I was just three years old. Is the twig really bent that early?

We used to say that no one likes a show-off, but then I think about the ways in which social networks and online video sites enable those who crave attention to turn themselves into minor celebrities. "There's no *I* in *team*," said one sportswriter to another. "But there is an *m* and an *e.*"

A professor named Arthur Bell has written a book titled *How to Write Attention-Getting Memos, Letters, and E-mails,* a guide for business writers. On the cover, "Attention-Getting" appears in the largest letters. "Most of us swim in a sea of poor writing styles," writes Bell, so the competition for attention is great.

"To explain art we need to attend to attention," writes Brian Boyd in *On the Origin of Stories,* his study of how evolution resulted in a species of narrative-obsessed beings called humans. "Shared attention is the first essential ingredient" of empathy, writes the psychologist Daniel Goleman. "As two people attend to what the other says and does, they generate a sense of mutual interest, a joint focus that amounts to perceptual glue."

As a writer, I want to create that glue, but before I can get you to stick to me as a reader, I must gain your attention. One way to keep your attention is to promise you something short and valuable. In effect, I tell the reader: This will not waste your time. It will have a power disproportionate to its modest length. You will be better off having read it.

Having focused on the *how* of writing short, we now turn in part 2 to the *why.* The good and responsible writer works from a sense of mission and purpose, no matter how short the text. We discover in these next chapters that over centuries and even millennia, the purposes attached to short writing have remained constant. From tombstone to tattoo, from telegram to tweet, from speech balloon to skywriting, from T-shirt to bumper sticker, from sonnet to personal ad, we visit writers at work, striving to perfect their craft.

23

Enshrine.

A much overlooked canvas for short writing is the human body. Think of the scene in a bar when a young woman writes her phone number on the back of a suitor's hand. Think of the reporter who does not want to call attention by writing in a notebook and surreptitiously scribbles the name of a source on her palm. Think of all those sailors with the names of sweethearts inked on their arms. The reporter Ben Montgomery has "Truth" tattooed on his forearm. My choice would be "Ambiguity," or maybe, in the era of Wikipedia, "Disambiguation."

When Casey Anthony was on trial in Orlando in 2011 for the murder of her young daughter, much was made of a tattoo Casey purchased in the days after her child disappeared. On her left shoulder appear the words "Bella Vita," Italian for "Good Life." In the absence of a definite or indefinite article, it was not clear whether the words should be translated "*The* Good Life," a celebration of her newfound freedom without a daughter to care for, or "*A* Good Life," in memory of her lost daughter.

"The body may be a temple," wrote Bryan Kirk, out of Harker Heights, Texas, "but it can also be a canvas, and to some a walking memorial." Kirk reported on soldiers who have the names of fallen comrades tattooed on their bodies. Staff Sergeant Chris Maust wears eighteen names of the dead: "Eighteen dog tags with the names of the men he called friends form a semicircle on his back and outline an image of a Cavalry Stetson placed on the butt of a rifle buried in a pair of cavalry boots."

When Nick Schuyler survived a boat accident in the Gulf of Mexico that killed three of his friends, part of his emotional recovery included a memorial of ink on his right arm. The image of a cross and anchor frames the initials of his dead friends and the passage "In the hour of adversity, be not without hope."

Just as it is expensive and painful to remove a tattoo, there is a certain permanence implied by carving a message onto metal or into stone. That practice is as old as written language itself, which explains, I suppose, our fascination with cemeteries. Phil Spector, the famous song producer (now in prison for murder), recorded a memorable rock ballad titled "To Know Him Is to Love Him." They were the words carved on the gravestone of his father, who killed himself in 1949, when Phil was just nine years old.

Here is a list of famous epitaphs culled from the website 2Spare.com:

- "My Jesus mercy." (Al Capone)
- "The best is yet to come." (Frank Sinatra)
- "That's all folks" (Mel Blanc; the epitaph is the trademark line of the cartoon character Porky Pig, whose voice was provided by Blanc for many years)
- "Don't try." (Charles Bukowski, American poet, daring anyone tempted to deface his gravestone with bad rhyme)
- "She did it the hard way." (Bette Davis)
- "I had a lover's quarrel with the world." (Robert Frost)
- "Hey Ram." (Oh God.) (Mahatma Gandhi)
- "Free at last. Free at last. Thank God Almighty I'm free at last." (Martin Luther King Jr.)
- "Curiosity did not kill this cat." (Studs Terkel)
- "Against you I will fling myself unvanquished and unyielding, O Death!" (Virginia Woolf)

What I find most interesting among these epitaphs is their variety in length, form, and tone. The shortest is two words (Gandhi); the longest eleven (Woolf). We have a complete sentence in the first person (Frost), an exclamatory apostrophe against Death (Woolf), an imperative warning (Bukowski), and a quotation from a Negro spiritual (King). In tone, look at the difference between the penitential hope of Capone and the slangy confidence of that cool cat Studs Terkel.

The creative choices within short writing are made manifest by these differences, even though their purpose is the same: to mark the passing of a life into death. Some headstones display prayers, poems, songs, excerpts, or pieces of oratory. Some epitaphs are solemn, others playful; some use wordplay, others abstractions; some are borrowed, others are new; some are in the voice of the dead, others of the living.

As I was thinking of the grammar and rhetoric of epitaphs, I received a message from an old college friend, Joe Morrissey. His younger brother, Bill Morrissey, had been found dead in a Georgia motel room, having lost a long battle against alcoholism. I had never met Bill, but I knew him through Joe as a remarkably creative person. That creativity would lead to a career as an author, songwriter, and prominent folk balladeer. A couple of hundred friends and admirers, many of them musicians, showed up in a New Hampshire meadow to celebrate Bill's life and musical legacy. The family would bury Bill in that meadow and were trying to figure out how the headstone would read. They wanted words, after all, for a man of the word. Joe asked if I would help.

This seemed like a special challenge, capturing the spirit of a man in a handful of unrevisable words. When we speak about the tentative nature of language, we often use the truism "It's not written in stone, after all." But what if it *is* to be written in stone?

Rounder Records had issued a collection of Bill's best work, so my first thought was to listen to Bill's voice and to hear and then study his lyrics. From twenty songs, I selected eighteen lyrics, a goodly number. Bill, it turns out, wrote songs about the bottle, death, and the afterlife, and even his worldly tunes have a forward momentum, a sense that the narrator is headed somewhere — for better or worse. I picked out my favorites:

- "I can't believe it gets this cold in Barstow."
- "He'd cross the other side."
- "I quit keeping score."
- "I think I'll take a nap."
- "Finally paid his tab and kept a dollar for the toll."
- "The dog can't move no more."
- "It's a great life when you're dead."
- "I'm going steady with Patsy Cline."
- "I bought Robert Johnson a beer."
- "Get out while you can."
- "You'll never get to heaven if you don't stop talking."
- "I couldn't stay long here in the land of snow."
- "I've been long gone."

The family curated this list, along with other suggestions, to decide on the words that would keep Bill's spirit alive, long after this generation has passed, long after we are dust in the wind. In the end, the family chose the last suggestion on my list and extended it to include the entire verse:

BILL MORRISSEY

SINGER, SONGWRITER, NOVELIST

1951–2011

"I'VE BEEN LONG GONE

FROM THE STAGE TO THE HIGHWAY

TO THE NIGHT GRILLE

AND EVERYWHERE I WENT

TIME JUST STOOD STILL."

One final lesson. I was visiting a town in Texas during the spring of 2012 and stayed at a hotel along a riverfront. The young clerk there wore a white scarf that almost concealed a tattoo on the side of her neck that extended along the length of her jawline. It was black text, framed with red decoration. I looked more closely and discovered it to be a man's name inked in elaborate Gothic script: "Roderick." I have a tattoo of a heart and my wife's name, "Karen," but it's near my shoulder, and I got it when I was sixty-two years old. You'd really have to love a guy, and be committed to him for the long haul, to tattoo his name across your carotid artery. What would happen if you broke up or divorced? Then I noticed it. The red lines were not decoration but a rectangle with the word "Void," which now defaced Roddy's once-honored name. "Roderick Void." There are times when you can't omit needless words, even in the smallest of texts. And you can't delete them. Or conceal them. Or laser them off. Sometimes all you can do is stamp them "Void."

GRACE NOTES

1. In your reading and writing, begin to notice examples of short writing used to honor and enshrine. Collect some examples in your daybook and offer your impressions or interpretations of those texts.

2. The next time you visit a cemetery, linger awhile to study the epitaphs. Most of these will be written by formula ("Beloved father"), but some will be strikingly original ("Best damn dad"). Record the ones that stand out from the rest.

3. *The Word Made Flesh,* edited by Eva Talmadge and Justin Taylor, is a remarkable collection of literary tattoos. Why would a young woman from Boston tattoo the Latin phrase "Non sum qualis eram" across her midsection? It means "I am not what I once was." Look for the signs people have written on their skin as potential details that define character.

4. Write a fictional vignette about a person who gets a tattoo he or she later regrets.

24

~~~

Crack wise.

When Shakespeare wrote that brevity was the soul of wit, he might have been chastising a friend of mine who relishes the attention that comes from telling long jokes. Long, long jokes. This sit-down comedian also laughs at his own jokes at an exaggerated decibel level. He then looks at me in disbelief when I don't laugh. "Wasn't worth the wait," I suggest.

My friend should read the work of the satirist Andy Borowitz, such as this gem:

> CUPERTINO, Calif.—A scientific study released today says that iPad owners are less likely to commit adultery "because they stop noticing other people altogether." According to the study, commissioned by Apple Inc., iPad use disrupts what scientists agree are the necessary

first stages of extramarital sex: "noticing, admiring, and talking to other people."

The study, on a sample of 1,000 iPad owners, found that not only did iPad use make them uninterested in extramarital sex, "their nonstop talking about the amazing features and apps make them completely unattractive to potential sex partners as well."

For the record, the author turns that literary trick—a critique of the mediated culture enabled by mobile devices—in a mere ninety-four words.

Much shorter are the edgy one-liners delivered by the actor-comic Zach Galifianakis, as captured in *Rolling Stone* magazine:

- "Remember the kid who had sex with his high school teacher? I heard on the news today that he died. Apparently he died of high-fiving."
- "I have a lot of growing up to do. I realized that the other day inside my fort."

So what makes something funny? Is there such a thing as a grammar of humor? To even ask such questions threatens to turn Porky Pig into Pokey Prig. But there are obvious strategies that go into the making of a good joke, the two most important of which are the *buildup* and the *punch line*.

We recognize the *buildup* with the appearance of certain stock characters in the world of jokes. "A man walked into a bar wearing a duck on his head. The bartender served him a

scotch and soda and handed him a check for $7.50. 'We don't need the check,' quacked the duck. 'I've already got the bill.'"
The man with the duck on his head; the bartender; the traveling salesman; the farmer's daughter. Adding structure and predictability to the buildup is the repetition of three: "A priest, a rabbi, and a minister were riding in a small airplane, when the plane hit some turbulence..."

The buildup only works, of course, if there is a payoff at the end in the form of a *punch line,* which is sometimes only a punch phrase or even a punch word. The first Galifianakis joke above ends with "high-fiving." Another ends with "inside my fort," which provides the punch of the story. Notice what happens if we invert the word order: "I realized the other day inside my fort that I have a lot of growing up to do." That inversion gives us a statement with a bit of tension between part one and part two, but not a joke. If there is a universal strategy for cracking wise, it would be to save the good stuff until the end.

Here's the feature writer and columnist Gene Weingarten:

I learned to write humor almost entirely from Dave Barry, whom I hired and then edited for years. Once, I impulsively asked Dave if there was any rhyme or reason to what he did, any writing rules that he followed. The questions surprised both of us; he and I were never much for rules or strictures or limits or templates. Eventually, he decided yes, there was actually one modest principle that he'd adopted almost unconsciously: "I try to put the funniest word at the end of the sentence."

He's so right. I stole that principle from him, and have shamelessly made it my own. When asked today whether there are any good rules for writing humor, I say "Always try to put the funniest word at the end of your sentence underpants."

Let's test the "underpants" rule in these examples from the *Washington Post,* which challenged readers to "take any word from the dictionary, alter it by adding, subtracting or changing one letter, and supply a new definition." These winners crack me up:

- "Ignoranus: A person who's both stupid and an asshole."
- "Reintarnation: Coming back to life as a hillbilly. "

Whatever the length of the sentence, the joke hits its mark when the writer places the odd, interesting, or startling word at the end. So perhaps Shakespeare was wrong. Perhaps it is not brevity that serves as the soul of wit, but emphatic word order.

As we know from our own malapropisms, humor can be just as funny when it is the product of inadvertence as when it is the result of a crafted plan. Here, for example, are sentences that supposedly appeared in high school book reports or term papers. Notice that, in addition to emphatic word order, the humor is generated by the juxtaposition of things that seem odd or out of balance when placed next to each other:

- "The ballerina rose gracefully en pointe and extended one slender leg behind her, like a dog at a fire hydrant."

- "He was deeply in love. When she spoke, he thought he heard bells, as if she were a garbage truck backing up."
- "Her face was a perfect oval, like a circle that had its two sides gently compressed by a Thighmaster."

What a surprise to look up and see news bloopers such as this one inscribed on the bathroom walls of the Washington, DC, Newseum:

Newspaper correction from the *Rutland (Vt.) Herald:* A story on Sally Ann Carey Thursday incorrectly stated that the family of a missing girl came to her for a psychic consultation. Two friends of the girl came to that session, and later Carey talked with the girl's mother. Also, Carey worked for Rutland Mental Health, not the Rutland Regional Medical Center. She taught swimming, not singing, adopted one child, not two, and at times contacts healing guides, not healing gods.

Not a single example in this chapter rises to the sophistication of humor as art. There is no sight of the members of the Algonquin Round Table and their pun competition ("You can lead a horticulture, but you can't make her think"), or the icy antilogic of a Noel Coward ("I have a memory like an elephant. In fact, elephants often consult me"), or the obscene rebellion against authority in a Lenny Bruce monologue ("If Jesus had been killed twenty years ago, Catholic school children would be wearing little electric chairs around their necks instead of crosses").

As I consider all these examples—brainy or crude, cool

or hot, social commentary or shots below the belt—it is helpful to see what they have in common: in addition to the underpants strategy (squirting the seltzer bottle at the end), we find surprising juxtapositions (schoolchildren and electric chairs), hyperbole (elephants consult Noel Coward), puns and other forms of wordplay (Dorothy Parker's "whore to culture"), and the perverse power of taking things to their illogical conclusion.

GRACE NOTES

1. Conduct a Google search of "the world's funniest jokes." As you read them, notice the pattern described by Dave Barry and Gene Weingarten, that the laugh-provoking word almost always comes at the end. Can you find exceptions?

2. Humor is often rendered in short forms, and not everyone has the wit to write it. No matter. One value of brief texts, including jokes, is that they can be borrowed. If you want your own prose to be lighter and brighter, embed within it the best examples of humor you have collected from other sources. With attribution, of course.

3. In addition to emphatic word order, humor in short forms often depends on the juxtaposition of two things or two people that don't belong together. Think of it as the *Buffy the Vampire Slayer* effect. My high school rock band was called T. S. and the Eliots. Keep notes in your daybook of the humorous collisions you encounter in the world: a dentist with bad teeth, a chiropractor from Cairo, a stripper who works days as a copy editor.

25

Sound wise.

On most days I'd prefer being a wise guy to being a wise man, but what the shallow joke and the deep proverb share is brevity. On many occasions a bit of wisdom can be dispensed extemporaneously in a conversation or a message, as when the editor Gene Patterson advised journalists: "Don't just make a living, make a mark." Or when Nelson Poynter told an interviewer, "I'd rather be a newspaper editor than the richest man in the world."

Much more often, the wise sentence or short passage is selected from a much longer text and often ripped from its original context. A famous example comes from the Chicago newspaper columnist Finley Peter Dunne, who wrote in the voice of an Irish bartender at the end of the nineteenth century. It is from one of his columns that journalists today might express the idea that the mission of newspapers is to "afflict the comfortable, and comfort the afflicted." While that is what Dunne wrote, it is not what he meant. In its original setting, the phrase was part of a list of examples of things that proved the overreaching *arrogance* of newspapers in pretending to be all things to all people:

> Th' newspaper does ivrything f'r us. It runs th' polis foorce an' th' banks, commands th' milishy, controls th' ligislachure, baptizes th' young, marries th' foolish, comforts th' afflicted, afflicts th' comfortable, buries th' dead an' roasts thim aftherward.

One of the underappreciated forms of wisdom literature is the advice column, and the most profound of these was written by Abraham Cahan, the longtime editor of the New York City newspaper the *Jewish Daily Forward*. In 1906, Cahan invented a genre known in Yiddish as a Bintel Brief, advice designed to help millions of Jewish immigrants face the challenges of a new life in America. Letters came to him with problems about love, marriage, family life, religion, politics, and money, and his answers were almost always wise, practical, sympathetic — and short.

One early letter comes from a self-described "freethinker" who wants to marry a girl from an Orthodox Jewish family. Her parents want her to have a religious wedding and insist that the groom come to the synagogue. To which Cahan responds:

> The advice is that there are times when it pays to give in to old parents and not grieve them. It depends on the

circumstances. When one can get along with kindness it is better not to break off relations with the parents.

On another occasion, Cahan receives a remarkable letter from a writer who signs it "The Newborn." This young husband tells a poignant story about how he had suffered with a wife who was very ill, how he was torn about taking care of her at home or rushing back to the factory so he would not be fired. In a moment of despair, he lay beside her and opened the gas jet, expecting that death would bring an end to their suffering. But she was revived, and after two weeks in the hospital, she was well. "Now I am happy that we are alive, but I keep thinking of what almost happened to us. Until now I never told anyone about it, but it bothers me. I have no secrets from my wife, and I want to know whether I should now tell her all, or not mention it. I beg you to answer me."

Cahan's answer:

The letter depicting the sad life of the worker is more powerful than any protest against the inequality between rich and poor. The advice to the writer is that he should not tell his wife that he almost ended both their lives. This secret may be withheld from his beloved wife, since it is clear he keeps it from her out of love.

At first I was struck by the formality of these responses, best exhibited by Cahan's using the third person rather than directing the response to the letter writer. In a 1929 memoir, quoted in the book *A Bintel Brief* by Isaac Metzker, Cahan explains his mission and purpose: "People often need the opportunity to be able to pour out their heavy-laden hearts. Among our immigrant masses this need was very marked. Hundreds of thousands of people, torn from their homes and their dear ones, were lonely souls who thirsted for expression, who wanted to hear an opinion, who wanted advice in solving their weighty problems. The 'Bintel Brief' created just this opportunity for them."

I sense a wonderful tension here between the voice of the letter writers, which is intensely personal, soulful, and narrative in nature, and the voice of the wise and sympathetic responder, whose more formal prose suggests some level of authority and wisdom and allows the writer to address not just the person with the problem but the entire community.

About the same time that Abe Cahan was writing advice to husbands and wives on the Lower East Side of Manhattan, an Englishwoman named Blanche Ebbutt began offering her book of "don'ts" for married couples. Her advice to husbands includes the following:

- "Don't try to keep bad news from your wife. She will guess that something is wrong, and will worry far more than if you tell her straight out."
- "Don't expect your wife to hold the same views as yours on every conceivable question. Some men like an echo, it is true, but it becomes very wearisome in time."
- "Don't let ambition crowd out love. There ought to be room for both in your life, but some men are so busy 'getting on' that they have no time to make love to their wives."

As for wives, Lady Ebbutt advises: "Don't grumble because your husband insists on wearing an old coat in the house. He wears it because it is the most comfortable garment he possesses, and home is the place for comfort." (I'm beginning to love this woman.) "Don't say that golf is a selfish game, and a married man ought to give it up. You learn to play, and then join a mixed club; your husband will be only too delighted to have you with him. But don't make up your mind that you could never like the game until you've tried it. Never mind if you don't become a crack player; the main thing is to derive pleasure from community of interest." (It's official: I love her.) While this book has been republished for its quaintness, it retains a progressive view of the partnership of marriage, inspired no doubt by the growing political power of women early in the last century.

Another fascinating subgenre of wisdom literature — wisdom at its most practical — is the rule of thumb. Tom Parker, the author of a collection titled *Rules of Thumb,* describes such a rule as "a homemade recipe for making a guess. It is an easy-to-remember guide, somewhere between a mathematical formula and a shot in the dark. A farmer, for instance, knows to plant his corn when oak leaves are the size of squirrels' ears." Here are a few rules of thumb, first published in the magazine *CoEvolution Quarterly:*

- "The rain is over when dry spots appear on the blacktop."
- "If you find one error while proofreading, there are likely to be several more in the same or contiguous paragraphs."

- "Jogging burns about 100 calories per mile."
- "Good hashish should make you cough on the first hit."
- "Don't pay more than twice your annual income on a house."

To be memorable, usable on a whim, the rule of thumb must have fewer than thirty words. Hey, I think I just created a rule of thumb!

GRACE NOTES

Wisdom literature comes in a rich variety of short forms, as indicated by this paraphrase of a taxonomy found in the *American Heritage Dictionary:*

- *Saying:* "an often repeated and familiar expression": "America is a land of opportunity."
- *Maxim:* "an expression of a general truth or a rule of conduct": "It's not the size of the wand, it's the skill of the magician."
- *Adage:* a saying that gains strength from long use: "Good things come in small packages."
- *Saw:* a saying that has become trite from overuse: "You can't take it with you."
- *Motto:* a phrase that describes the guiding principles of a person, profession, or institution: "Semper fidelis" (U.S. Marine Corps, "Always faithful").
- *Epigram:* "a witty expression, often paradoxical and brilliantly phrased," as when Samuel Johnson called remarriage "a triumph of hope over experience."

- *Proverb:* "an old and popular saying" that offers practical wisdom or advice: "Slow and steady wins the race."
- *Aphorism:* "a concise expression of truth," deep in content, and offered with unquestioned authority: "You must be the change you wish to see in the world" (Mahatma Gandhi).

In your daybook, try your hand at mastering the aphorism. Test your efforts against the criteria established by James Geary in *The World in a Phrase.* His five laws of the aphorism are: "It must be brief. It must be personal. It must be definitive. It must be philosophical. It must have a twist."

26

Sell.

I can't think of a better example of short writing than this one: a sign that reads For Sale. We stick it on our cars, houses, and boats. Even those who have no interest in buying that 1965 Mustang convertible now see the object in a different light. Remember the six-word story inspired by the classified ads: "For sale: baby shoes, never worn"?

America is a country of sellers, an archetype expressed often in literature and popular culture, from the mountebank selling snake oil; to Willy Loman in *Death of a Salesman* by Arthur Miller; to the traveling salesman who seduces the farmer's daughter and steals her wooden leg in Flannery O'Connor's "Good Country People"; to the protagonist of Meredith Willson's *Music Man;* to the carnival barker with his come-on. "Step right up, folks, and see Little Egypt do her famous Dance of the Pyramids," begins a classic song by the Coasters. Now "she walks, she talks, she crawls on her belly like a reptile. Just one thin dime. One-tenth of a dollar. Step right up, folks."

Think of all the things we sell: used cars, hot dogs in the stadium, life insurance policies, cemetery plots, aluminum siding, the services of streetwalkers and ambulance chasers, lots of drugs, and lots and lots of guns, both legal and illegal.

Most of all, we sell ourselves. Even if we don't sell ourselves short, we sell ourselves in short forms. Take as exhibit A the humble T-shirt.

I probably own about twenty T-shirts and wear them to sleep in, to mow the lawn, to walk around the park, the most casual and common sartorial purposes. You could probably read my T-shirts and take from their messages a general sense of who I am, or think I am, or want to be. In other words, I'm using this short writing to sell an image of myself, to both friends and strangers. In my case, you'd see references to sports teams, theatrical productions I favor, pizza joints I frequent, and plays on words I enjoy. (Baseball, music, pizza, and language. That's me.)

It's December and I'm reading an endless number of holiday catalogs, many of which sell T-shirts. Here are some of my favorites:

> i before e
> except after c
> weird?

My Indian Name
Is
"Sleeps with Dog"

I Totally Agree
With Myself

If life gives you melons,
You might be dyslexic.

The
Hokey Pokey Clinic
A place to turn yourself around

Without Music Life would B♭

Quantum Mechanics
The dreams stuff is made of

Most of these shirts use images as well as words, usually with a clever connection between them, as in the shirt with the words "I Need My Space" above a picture of the solar system, a tiny arrow pointing to Earth; or the caption "Treble Maker" under a G-clef symbol; or an image of two atoms talking to each other: one says, "I think I lost an electron," and the other answers, "Are you positive?"

More common than such creative clothing, of course, is the T-shirt carrying the college logo or the product signifier, such as the Nike swoosh along with the encouragement "Just do it." Such an artifact reminds us that no subgenre is more important to the literature of selling than the slogan.

The etymology of the word *slogan,* "a phrase expressing the aims or nature of an enterprise, organization, or candidate," is revealing. Its etymon is Gaelic and translates to "battle cry," especially as employed by the berserkers in Scottish clans. The slogan, then, is not a rational conclusion of a subtle argument. The slogan is in your face, a call to arms.

Laurence Urdang and Celia Dame Robbins edited a book titled *Slogans,* which they describe as "a collection of more than 6,000...rallying cries and other exhortations used in advertising, political campaigns, popular causes and movements, and divers efforts to urge people to take action." Such short phrases are designed to persuade readers to move, to sell them on a product, service, idea, political party, person, institution, team, celebrity, issue, or cause.

From the texts of bumper stickers alone, we could make a case for the continuing importance of the slogan to our political and civic life. Thousands of bumper stickers are created each year on subjects related to American politics and culture, and many are created by companies that also print and sell T-shirts. In other words, the bumper sticker is a T-shirt for an automobile. As in this pro–Sarah Palin message: "You Can Keep 'The Change'/Palin 2012." Or this negative one: "Sarah Palin 2012/The world's supposed to end anyway."

In case you are wondering who invented the slogan, it may have been Moses (maybe he slapped a message on the back of a chariot). Urdang and Robbins remind us that you'd have to take a long ride on the Wayback Machine to find the earliest examples in human culture. They list:

- "Let my people go." (Exodus 5:1)
- "Know thyself." (from the oracle at Delphi)
- "Love thy neighbor as thyself."
- "Liberté! Égalité! Fraternité!" (Liberty! Equality! Fraternity!, the rallying cry of the French Revolution)

These product and business slogans, according to Urdang and Robbins, are so powerful that they have endured as part of American culture:

- "Breakfast of Champions" (Wheaties)
- "99 44/100% Pure" (Ivory soap)
- "Cover the Earth" (Sherwin-Williams paint)
- "His Master's Voice" (RCA Victor)
- "Think" (IBM)
- "When It Rains It Pours" (Morton salt)

I did a spontaneous research tour around my office and put my coworkers on the spot: "Name a product slogan. Quick." I have witnesses to testify that these examples were chosen spontaneously and at random, yet a bit of light reverse engineering will reveal the fifteen different methods used to seal the deal:

1. "L.S./M.F.T." ("Lucky Strike means fine tobacco"; an abbreviation, using initials)
2. "You'll wonder where the yellow went when you brush your teeth with Pepsodent." (iambic meter and rhyme)
3. "Ring around the collar." (Whisk detergent; an embarrassing problem to be solved)

4. "Bet you can't eat just one." (Lay's potato chips; an implied monologue, one kid daring another)
5. "Eat Mor Chikin." (Chick-fil-A; cows who can't spell)
6. "M'm! M'm! Good!" (Campbell's soup; the effect of using the product)
7. "I'm lovin' it." (McDonald's; first-person testimony)
8. "See the USA in your Chevrolet." (implied patriotism)
9. "Good mood food." (Arby's; assonance and rhyme)
10. "I wish I were an Oscar Mayer weiner." (words from a musical jingle)
11. "You want to know what comes between me and my Calvins? Nothing." (sexual innuendo)
12. "The Real Thing." (Coke; three one-syllable words)
13. "Rock the Vote." (MTV; juxtaposing two surprising elements)
14. "Santa has elves. You have Target." (practical demythology)
15. "With a name like Smucker's, it has to be good." (my all-time favorite, a naughty Yiddish joke posing as self-deprecation)

Wow. That's an impressive list, one that reveals the rich variety of writing strategies available to the author of what is, most often, a single sentence.

Notice how many of these slogans stand in support of a brand name. It is that name that represents one of the shortest high-stakes writing forms of all. So much depends on the answer to this question: What will I name my product? In his worthy book *Microstyle*, Christopher Johnson reveals some of the tricks of the trade when it comes to the creation of brand names such as Pentium, PowerBook, BlackBerry, Swiffer, and Febreze:

> Names don't just represent brands; they *start* brands. The ideas and feelings that a name evokes provide the scaffolding for a brand. Consider the name Google. Even if you don't know it's based on *googol*, a word coined by a child for a very large number, you probably get a playful, almost goofy vibe from it. Maybe you associate it (consciously or not) with the cartoon character Barney Google, the expression "googly eyes," or representations of baby talk like "goo goo ga ga." Now think of how well that vibe goes with Google's simple interface, the primary colors of its logo, and its reputation as a fun and creative place to work. Now try to imagine the same logo and reputation being associated with the name Microsoft.

In a world so influenced by information companies such as Google, Microsoft, and Yahoo! each writer looks for opportunities to turn his or her byline into a brand.

GRACE NOTES

It does no good for the poet or essayist to look down on the writer of advertising copy. All writers can learn from specialized practitioners of the craft, and ad writing requires a keen sense of audience and purpose. After all, the purpose is the purchase. Consider, for example, this advice from *The Adweek Copywriting Handbook,* by Joseph Sugarman. For this veteran, no element of copy is too small, including typeface, paragraph headings, and white space. The first sentence must be short, compelling, and easy to read. "Almost as important as the first," the second sentence is an invitation to keep reading. His checklist of persuasive elements includes the following:

- A clear product explanation
- New features
- Technical language for credibility
- Resolving objections
- Gender preference
- Clarity and rhythm
- Product service (what happens when it breaks?)
- Trial period
- Price comparison
- Testimonial
- How to order now

What we have here is an elaborate formula for a text that might come in at one hundred words or fewer, in some ways as precise and exacting as the sonnet. If this seems like hackwork, just catch some episodes of the popular television series *Mad Men,* about the Madison Avenue advertising industry in the 1960s. Then treat yourself to a two-martini lunch.

Try your hand at writing an ad for your favorite local restaurant, drawing strategies from Sugarman's list above. Is your ad persuasive? Test it by showing it to someone who has never eaten there before. You might wind up with a lunch date.

27

Entice.

The publisher of Little, Brown is Michael Pietsch, and when he approved of this project he sent my editor, Tracy Behar, a note that included the affirmation that we indeed live in an era when short writing is increasingly important. Michael offered a number of examples, none more surprising than the profiles written by subscribers of dating sites, such as Match.com and Cupid.com.

Through my research on these sites—OK, I kinda signed up for a couple—I've learned that these "advertisements for self" run from one hundred to three hundred words. Along the way, I stumbled upon how to write these profiles well. The success of the method can be measured by the quality and quantity of the matches you receive. The best profiles seem to follow a three-part structure:

> *The Pitch:* Where the writer attempts to stand apart from the masses in a sentence or two at the top.
> *The Lure:* Where the writer compiles evidence (anecdotes, preferences, humor) that he is worthy.
> *The Catch:* Where the writer ends with an irresistible call to action.

In an attempt to learn this form, I decided to write a pitch for myself (without publishing it until now). Everything in it is true except for the make-believe aspect of looking for love. (In fact, I've been married for more than forty-one years to the world's most grumpy yet desirable woman. As they said about John Lennon in the early days of the Beatles: "Sorry, girls, he's married.")

The Pitch

If you are looking to put a little music back in your life, I'm your guy. I'm not a professional singer or musician, but I love to sing while I play the piano or guitar, and a love song always sounds better if you have someone to sing it to. What's your favorite?

The Lure

I like relationships built on honesty, friendship, loyalty, and fun. It took me a while to learn, but I think I'm a pretty good listener. If we are at the dinner table and I sense you've had a bad day, I'll stop eating, look you straight in the eyes, and ask what's wrong—and how I can help.

  If we connect, I'll send you flowers, not just on Valentine's Day, but when you least expect it.

I've got a great job as a teacher and writer, and I own my own house not far from the Gulf of Mexico, where this weekend I'd love to hit the St. Pete Beach Seafood Festival, where one of my favorite bands—the Hunks of Funk—will be jammin'.

The Catch

I'm looking for someone not afraid to get a little sand between her toes while we're holding hands and watching another glorious Florida sunset, looking for rainbows and dolphins jumping. I've got lots of friends in town (including a golden retriever named Riley and a cat named Oz) but not that very special person. Not yet. Maybe it's you.

The task here is not unlike writing a 250-word essay designed to get you into the college of your choice. I've learned from admissions officers that the wise young writer will grab the attention of the reader in the first ten seconds, will project an authentic voice that sounds different from the voices of others, and will provide evidence to seal the deal, to make the readers say, "We need this kid in our school."

I read about fifty profiles from women, and the first thing I learned is that your user name is important, a form of short writing in and of itself. I did not understand this before I listed FluffyZorro as my handle, which sounds like the name of a backup singer for the Village People. So among the women who are supposedly ready to hear from me, there is suzy, Julie, love, jellybelly, lisa, pina, purplerose,

BethWithGreenEyes, cuttincutie, kisses48, sexpo, truevine, lovingheart, Filipina Heart, juicygem, twinklestarmama, and sandspur 007.

(Please don't judge me too harshly for confessing my preferences among these names. I must say I'd be curious about jellybelly for her willingness to take risks, BethWithGreenEyes for her good judgment in calling attention to her best feature, and twinklestarmama for... I have no idea. On the other hand, plain names strike me as too safe, and juicygem and sexpo scare the hell out of me. I am conflicted about sandspur 007. That number might make her a James Bond fan—good—but *sandspur* suggests she may be too sharp and clingy.)

In language and purpose, dating profiles are dressed-up and elongated versions of the personal ad. Some of the funniest and most whimsical personal ads are collected on the website Oddee.com:

- "I'm Lance! Let's go out!" would not seem that compelling an ad, except it was posted on a huge billboard, purchased by Lance's coworkers.
- A forty-one-year-old farmer created a message in a cornfield, using cornstalks to create letters that were fifty feet tall. It says he's looking for a "S.W.F. Got 2 ♥ Farm'n."
- How about this pitch from Swamp Frog: "Seeking hip, fashion forward Swine for long term relationship. Must be fun, flirty, speak French and know Karate. Must be flexible enough to mix it up. Like to have twins someday. If you are my match, let's talk." Contact Kermit@muppets.com.

- And then there is this from a man who seems to know exactly what he wants: "Single male seeks double-jointed supermodel who owns a brewery and grows her own pot. Access to free concert tickets a plus, as is having open minded twin sister!"

As spicy as these are, the standard statements by both men and women on dating sites are cautious, unspecific, and—when you read a bunch—generic and predictable (the same as those college entrance essays). You could throw them in the air and catch one, and it would be almost indistinguishable from any you'd pick up off the floor. Men, my women friends tell me, describe themselves inevitably as sincere, easygoing, with a dry sense of humor and a love of life and the outdoors (code for deer hunting with automatic weapons, ladies). They love Bruce Springsteen. Against all odds, they are looking for a woman "who is not high maintenance."

From women writers, a word cloud would surface these words and phrases: *About themselves,* they are caring, fun-loving, down to earth, compassionate; they love music, animals, walks on the beach, travel, and exploring new things. *About him,* they want someone who is honest, fit, romantic, motivated, caring, kindhearted, open minded, a "best friend" with a good heart and a good sense of humor.

The lack of specificity serves, no doubt, as a defense mechanism against clowns and perverts on the Internet, but also as a way to spread a wide net. A skeptical and strategic generality means there will be no deal breakers at the beginning of the process.

A good profile, I am now ready to argue, takes chances,

moving from the world of special objects, activities, and personalities to the world of ideas and values. The website iVillage.com offered this example as a model:

Username: 1in6Billion

Headline: A Barrel of Monkeys Has Nothing on Me

Vitals: Female, 35, Boston, MA

About Me:

Weird things happen to me: nothing that you should be afraid of, but just realize that if we get together, you're in for a wild ride. I've driven a go-kart for six laps with the back of the car in flames. My VW has broken down in front of a dozen honking customers in the drive-thru line at McDonald's (I've since upgraded to a better model). I work in public relations. I spend my days getting press coverage for people in the film and television industries, but the truth is, I'd rather be making my own headlines. My ultimate goal is to move to Los Angeles to be a writer/producer of feature films. Storytelling is my passion, but it won't be easy to leave my family behind because they are my anchor and the paradigm of everything that I aspire to be. I'm fortunate to have them in my life. Not to mention a legion of close friends from high school and college. I'm pragmatic but spontaneous. Nurturing but competitive. Peaceful but energetic. I love staying up late—whether it's to party, have sex or just read a good book—but I almost always sleep in on weekends. I definitely have an adventurous streak—whether it's trying out an exotic recipe in the kitchen, running with my dog or traveling the world thanks to my good friends at Orbitz and Priceline. My dream trip is taking the Orient Express from Paris to Venice to Budapest, then relaxing on a Greek island with nothing but sunscreen, James Patterson books and InStyle magazine. Are you in?

1in6Billion has exhausted me already, in just 264 words. But compared to others I've read, she is a revelation, a sensual, fun-loving, brainy goddess. If I were available and of her generation and region, I would probably want to know more. Among the things I find attractive: She's a good storyteller who likes to cook, travel, walk her dog, and fool around. The fact that she is ambitious—with specific goals and dreams—helps her to stand out, and her reluctance to leave family and friends makes her all the more human. In another world, another life, FluffyZorro would send her a message, telling her that I'm eager to enjoy more of her stories.

So in the digital age the dating profile turns out to be a socially significant form of short writing, a subgenre of the personal essay that has its own special requirements and the power to persuade.

GRACE NOTES

Why are the stakes so high for the profile in which you sell yourself? Because if it's well written, it can help get you into the college or job of your choice. In a social context, it can land you a date, even a potential spouse. It's a genre!

MidlifeBachelor.com offers the most thorough advice on how best to take advantage of the form. In summary:

1. Choose your user name carefully. (It's the first thing people see.)
2. Your heading, or catchphrase, is critical. (An enticement to read further.)
3. The first few lines will make or break you. (I call it the ten-second rule.)
4. Keep things brief and simple. (No more than 250 words.)
5. Check spelling and grammar. (Don't be judged for a lack of intelligence because you did not have the time or energy to check your work.)
6. Pay attention to the close. (Consider asking a question that invites a response.)

Although the advice in this chapter has focused on the dating profile, the strategies for writing a good one apply across other forms of writing. Reread one of your own essays and evaluate it against these questions: Is my title or headline compelling? Do I begin the text with something irresistibly interesting? Do I reward the reader throughout with incentives to keep reading? Does my ending make the reader glad he or she has arrived? Have I purged the text of distracting and misleading errors? And finally, would a reader of my work discover in my writing voice someone worth talking to over a beer or a cup of coffee? Everything you write is, in essence, a dating profile.

28

~~~~~

Surprise with content.

I must have been thinking about the enduring power of the Gettysburg Address during the 2012 Super Bowl. The New York Giants defeated the New England Patriots 21–17. Madonna performed an extravagant half-time show in which she, looking like Cleopatra in drag, was enthroned on a stage and drawn onto the field by what looked like a legion of Roman gladiators.

At the end of the first half, the Patriots led 10–9. We had already seen dozens of those expensive Super Bowl commercials, ads for cars, tech companies, soft drinks, beer, and, of course, Doritos — mininarratives featuring cute dogs, talking babies, and impossible women. Some were clever, some lame. More than once I scratched my head, trying to figure out what product was for sale.

Leading into half-time activities was an ad widely

considered the most interesting and effective of the season. You didn't recognize the voice of the narrator at first, but it was Clint Eastwood's. It turned out to be a two-minute Chrysler spot, but it was perceived as something more important and more powerful: a highly idealized statement about the fall and rise of the American auto industry as a symbol for a general revival of the American spirit.

I have chosen to include the text here—with my interpretation of what made it work—because it measured about 260 words, almost exactly the length of Lincoln's most famous oration. If the thesis of this book stands up—that we can build a bridge between old and new forms of effective short writing—then we should be able to recognize patterns across authors, rhetorical strategies, and purposes that stand 150 years apart.

The ad demonstrates the relative nature of defining length in a text. In the land of thirty-, sixty-, and ninety-second spots, the two-minute spot towers over the rest, the longest (and most expensive) of the lot. Yet in most other contexts, 260 words constitute not a water tower but a fire hydrant. From Lincoln to Eastwood, Americans love to be inspired by two-minute blasts of good writing.

Don't be surprised that my commentary (in brackets) is longer than the original text (in italics), proving only that good short writing often demands a level of attention that leads to more writing.

> *It's halftime.* [A brilliant opening. Two simple words, one a contraction, placed in the immediate context of television viewers watching the game.] *Both teams are in their locker*

rooms discussing what they can do to win this game in the second half. [American civic culture is saturated with sports metaphors, analogies, and allusions. While these can become clichéd and annoying, they are in context here.]

It's halftime in America, too. [Another sharp line, a riff off Reagan's "Morning in America" commercial, yet subtle enough that it does not signal that this will be a heavy-handed ideological piece.] *People are out of work and they're hurting. And they're all wondering what they're going to do to make a comeback. And we're all scared, because this isn't a game.* [This passage works as what the screenwriter Robert McKee calls an "inciting incident," an event that dramatically changes the way we see ourselves and the world. The incident is not specified, but no matter. We recognize it as an allusion to the collapse of the American economy, and all the damage it caused. No longer are we just watching a game. Now we are listening to a voice we recognize, a gritty voice we associate with the cowboy bravado of spaghetti Westerns or Dirty Harry aggression, but one that now echoes the coarse friction of a deep and protracted recession.]

The people of Detroit know a little something about this. They almost lost everything. But we all pulled together, now Motor City is fighting again. [We would expect the sentences to be short throughout, a strategy that builds dramatic and emotional tension. Here those short bits have a rhythm and variety that demand attention and move the narrative forward.]

I've seen a lot of tough eras, a lot of downturns in my life. [Suddenly the narrator is speaking in the first-person singular. He sounds like someone who has lived life and can speak with authority. The word *downturns* works hard here, standing for everything from personal failure and psychological depression to collective economic failure.] *And, times when we didn't understand each other. It seems like we've lost our heart at times. When the fog of division, discord, and blame made it hard to see what lies ahead.* [Notice the tactical shift from the first-person singular to the plural *we*—*e pluribus unum,* one out of many. That last verbless sentence (also called an intentional fragment) is the most rhetorical in the ad, with the simple metaphor of the fog followed by three allegorical villains: Division, Discord, and Blame. We are not in darkness, but in a fog, confused, trying to find our way. By implication the fog is never permanent. The fog lifts.]

But after those trials, we all rallied around what was right, and acted as one. [I think of this as fake history, the way we would have liked it to be. What could the writer be referring to? The Civil War? The Great Depression? Vietnam? Watergate? We never act as one, but that doesn't mean the language doesn't invite us to imagine that we could or should.] *Because that's what we do. We find a way through tough times, and if we can't find a way, then we'll make one.* [More propaganda, but I admire the way that last sentence resolves itself. "We'll make one" may seem like a general statement about finding solutions, but it also stands at the heart of a manufacturing economy. American needs to learn how to "make" things again, an evocation of what has been lost in Detroit and elsewhere throughout America.]

All that matters now is what's ahead. How do we come from behind? How do we come together? And, how do we win? [When a writer or speaker repeats a pattern (like those questions) three times, you know he or she is heading toward what dancers call the kick line. The first question and the third are metaphors of competition, but they frame the language of reconciliation.]

Detroit's showing us it can be done. And, what's true about them is true about all of us. [While the first half of the ad might be interpreted as having borrowed from the Republican playbook, here we are reminded that some unpopular policies of a Democratic administration bailed out America's automotive industry.]

This country can't be knocked out with one punch. We get right back up again and when we do the world is going to hear the roar of our engines. [My one negative response is to the needless shift from one sport to another, from football to boxing, and perhaps to stock car racing, if you can hear that in the roar of engines. That roar is meant to evoke the sound of industrial history, invention, and prosperity, from the transcontinental railroad to the postwar construction of the interstate highway system to the creation of muscle cars like the Mustang and Camaro to the sounds of fighter pilots and helicopters at war.]

Yeah, [Much better than *yes. Yeah* is the affirmation of the common man and woman and American child.] *it's halftime, America. And, our second half is about to begin.* [A strong ending, language that echoes the beginning, returns us to our American traditions of sports and competition, and implies that we are not at the end of the game — of the great American experiment — but smack-dab in the middle, with more greatness to come.]

I don't know how many Americans were present to hear Lincoln's two-minute address at the dedication of the cemetery at Gettysburg. Chrysler's two-minute spot, the work of the Oregon ad agency Wieden+Kennedy, was viewed by an audience of more than 110 million worldwide.

GRACE NOTES

1. Americans have a love/hate relationship with advertisements. We often find them obnoxious, especially when they interfere with our entertainment. The more popular the television show, it seems, the more endless the stream of commercials. On the other hand, certain ads not only gain our attention but become part of popular culture and even American history. Pay special attention to the ads that work. Focus on words, visuals, music, and imagery as they operate individually and together. What lessons can you draw for your own writing?

2. Watch and listen to the Chrysler ad on YouTube to test whether its approach stands up in the current state of the American economy. What gives an advertising message currency, and what elements make it feel dated?

3. Using the Chrysler ad as a model, write your own two-minute spot in support of a place or a cause you believe in.

29

‐‐‐‐

Reframe messages
as dialogue.

Even the young person who sends and receives hundreds of
text messages per day is unlikely to think of them as acts of
reading and writing—but they are. Most text messages,
including mine, are delivered in casual code for humdrum
purposes, a mode of expression that makes communication
seem as automatic as breathing:

ROY: coffee?
JEFF: now?
ROY: see u there
JEFF: k

But consider this exchange with my daughter Alison:

DAD: Ali, rock heaven has another saint. Janis greets Amy
   Winehouse.
ALISON: sad so sad. But not a surprise. I take comfort that she
   is free of that prison.

The twenty-seven words in these messages work hard.
Embedded in them is a story, a short biography of Amy
Winehouse. I deliver the news of the singer's death indirectly
and euphemistically, guessing that it is already known. I
allude to Janis Joplin and rock-and-roll heaven, connecting
Winehouse to a long tradition of fallen rockers. From Alison, we get judgments about the duration of the singer's suffering ("not a surprise") and its depth ("that prison"), a
metaphor for addiction.

All in twenty-seven words.

Such dialogue is neither dramatic nor Socratic, but it can
have its charms, as exemplified by the iPhone text-message
exchanges between me and my pal Tom French, each message captured in a word balloon. Juniper (or Junebug) is his
baby daughter, delivered by his wife Kelley at twenty-three
weeks, one pound, one ounce:

ROY: Merry Clark Christmas to the amazing French family.
   Hope that Juniper is reading the book we sent her [about
   Snooki from the reality TV show *Jersey Shore*]. We all
   need role models.
TOM: Merry Christmas, GoGo [my nickname—long story].
   Junebug has already devoured her Snooki book—literally.

And a few days later:

ROY: Didn't have my phone with me today so I couldn't wish my BFF a happy birthday. Hope your bride is providing celebratory sexual services.

TOM: Dang. Baby's messing w/my pimp daddy thang.... You want to come over for breakfast after church and then you and Sam and Kelley head for the gun range?

ROY: Wow what an offer. I am at Poynter on a writing jag. But tell Annie Oakley I will be up for it next time.

TOM: Godspeed, John Glenn.

On first blush, the drop from Socrates and Plato to Roy and Tom must feel all maximum velocity and hypergravitational, but using the secret code of friends, we, too, seek to puzzle together the meaning of life, love, literacy, lore, and friendship. The text-message exchange does what all good dialogue accomplishes in literature: reveals traits of character, advances a narrative, places the reader on the scene.

The narrative potential of the text message was revealed dramatically during the summer of 2011 when the world grieved the deaths of almost eighty Norwegians, most of them young. I remember being struck at the time by the redemptive power of the written word—but not just any written word. The killer, a thirty-two-year-old homegrown terrorist, had written lots of words, expressed in a fifteen-hundred-page logorrheic manifesto, years in the making and published on the Internet to explain his murderous rampage.

The question in such cases is always, why?

Like the Unabomber and other fanatics before him, Anders Behring Breivik used violence to voice a hatred that his words could never fully express. Those words, as excerpted by the world media, are nothing new. They echo the common complaint of political extremists, language that can be traced back to Nazi myths of the master race and beyond.

But this is not a book about bad long writing, so let's turn from Breivik's monster manifesto (which runs to roughly 300,000 words) to an exchange of text messages between sixteen-year-old Julie Bremnes and her mother, Marianne. According to the *Mail Online* and other sources, Julie and her friends heard shots on Utøya Island, ran to the shore, and sought cover behind an outcropping of rocks. From there she never saw the killer, but she could see the dead and wounded along the shore and the bodies of the dead floating on the water.

The text exchange between Julie and her mom, who was glued to her TV set, began at 5:42 p.m.:

JULIE: Mummy, tell the police that they must hurry. People are dying here!

MUM: I'm working on it, Julie. The police are coming. Dare you call me?

JULIE: No.

JULIE: Tell the police that there is a mad man running around and shooting people.

JULIE: They must hurry!

MUM: The police know it. This is not good, Julie. Police are calling us now. Give us a sign of life every five minutes, please?

JULIE: OK.

JULIE: We are surviving!

MUM: I understand, my girl. Stay in cover, do not move anywhere! The police are already on the way, if not already arrived! Do you see anyone injured or killed?

JULIE: We are hiding in the rocks along the coast.

MUM: Good! Should I ask your grandfather to come down and pick you up when everything is safe again? When you have the opportunity.

JULIE: Yes.

MUM: We will contact grandfather immediately.

JULIE: I love you even though I may shout a few times :)

JULIE: And I did not panic, even though I'm shit scared.

MUM: I know, my girl. We are awfully fond of you, too! Can you hear shots?

JULIE: No.

From television reports, the mom informs the daughter of what is going on, including that the gunman is disguised as a policeman. Mom uses the text messages to bolster her daughter's spirits and to inform her that help is near, including the final message about the police capture of the killer: "Now they have taken him!"

So great was the loss of life in Norway that the killer's words and actions will take their toll for years to come. How could they not? Let's just hope that the record of these events includes the dialogue between young Julie and her mother, an exchange that could be a scene in a Bergman film or an Ibsen play.

I take that back. The dramatic artists' representations are mere imitations of real life. (Now I'm channeling Plato!) This exchange feels more real, more human: from Julie's caring attention to others who are dying; to the reassurances mother and daughter provide each other; to the delivery of information that will keep Julie and her friends safe; to the gloriously Norwegian understatements of love; to the authenticity of the girl's fervent exclamation points, her slang that she is "shit scared," even history's best use of the smiley face.

I will lay this wager, that in the tsunami of words in the killer's manifesto, the reader will not find a single smiley face or any other tender expression of love for another. The text messages quoted above run 173 words and took minutes to write and exchange. The killer could have spent another decade writing, and used another 300,000 words, and never come close to the poignant power exchanged between mother and daughter, a love dispatch from a war front delivered in one of modernity's most common and casual media platforms with the irreplaceable energy of narrative to put us right there on the scene.

From the beginning, storytellers have embedded the work of other storytellers within their work. The story inside the story. The poets of heroic epics such as *Beowulf* or the *Odyssey* will describe scenes in which other poets are singing songs of other heroes long remembered. In the earliest novels, important truths were communicated in the form of letters from one character to another. In the age of electricity, those letters became telegrams or transcripts of telephone conversations. With each innovation of the digital age, the author has new opportunities to embed messages in reports and stories. What was once limited to dialogue can now be expressed in e-mails and text messages. As with dialogue, they can advance stories and reveal traits of character.

GRACE NOTES

1. Sit in a busy public space and eavesdrop on conversations. In your daybook, capture the most interesting snippets. Imagine a fictional scene in which that dialogue takes place.

2. Remember the distinctions between quotations and dialogue. Quotes are static and often explanatory, commenting on the action. Dialogue *is* action, helping to transport readers to another time and place, yet creating the illusion of the here and now.

3. Examine some threads of text messages exchanged between you and your friends. Capture one in your daybook, commenting not just on the text but on the subtext. Consider how much of the exchange is written in code.

4. Some of the first novels are called epistolary because the narrative is told in an exchange of letters between characters. In your daybook, experiment with a piece of short fiction in which the story is told through tweets or text messages.

30

~~~

Marry words with pictures.

There is no more underdeveloped form of short writing than the photo caption and cutline. Here Jeffrey Page of the *Record* in New Jersey shows the storytelling potential of the form. Frank Sinatra had just died, so imagine a one-column photo of him from the waist up. He's wearing a tux with a black bow tie. He's got a mike in his hand. He's obviously singing:

> If you saw a man in a tux and black bow tie swagger on stage like an elegant pirate, and if you had been told he would spend an hour singing Cole Porter, Gershwin, and Rodgers and Hart, and if when he opened his mouth you heard a little of your life in his voice, and if you saw his body arch back on the high notes (the ones he insisted you hear and feel and live with him), and if his swing numbers made you want to bounce and be happy and be

young and be carefree, and if when he sang "Try a Little Tenderness" and got to the line about a woman's wearing the same shabby dress it made you profoundly sad, and if years later you felt that his death made you a little less alive, you must have been watching this man who started as a saloon singer in Hoboken and went on to become the very definition of American popular music.

How can you write a 167-word caption without using the dead man's name? Page explains: "I know, I know, it violates every damned rule. Screw it....If you're a U.S. paper, and especially if you happen to be in New Jersey, you don't have to tell people that they're looking at a picture of Sinatra and not Mother Teresa."

Let's look at a very different style of captioning taken from a 1946 edition of the *Audubon Bird Guide: All the Birds of Eastern and Central North America*. I picked out from the collection of images and descriptions one of the only birds I can easily recognize, one that shows up regularly on Florida golf courses to observe my abysmal play: the roseate spoonbill. Here is the text by Richard H. Pough:

Identification: The adults, with their wholly pink wings and outstretched heads, are very distinctive in flight. Young are at first entirely white except for a touch of pink under the wings and on the tail. They become increasingly pink with age and are fully adult when 3 years old.

That forty-nine-word paragraph is delivered in what some scholars of rhetoric refer to as the classic style. In a persuasive text titled *Clear and Simple as the Truth*, Professors Francis-Noël Thomas and Mark Turner argue that

> classic style is focused and assured. Its virtues are clarity and simplicity; in a sense, so are its vices. It declines to acknowledge ambiguities, unessential qualifications, doubts, or other styles. It declines to acknowledge that it is a style. It makes its hard choices silently and out of the reader's sight. Once made, those hard choices are not acknowledged to be choices at all; they are presented as if they were inevitable because classic style is, above all, a style of presentation with claims to transparency.

Among their many examples of the classic style, Thomas and Turner hold up the *Audubon Guide* as a paragon, a work that manages to turn expert knowledge into an exchange with a knowledgeable friend, an encounter without slang or digression, a "conversation" with a passionate audience who will use new knowledge and put it into action, looking for wild birds.

When George Orwell noted that "good prose is like a windowpane," he was, mischievously no doubt, breaking his own rule, using a simile to illuminate his message, but also to call attention to the writer's style. How different, once again, is the *Audubon Guide*'s description of the habits of the sharp-shinned hawk:

> Years ago ornithologists called this a "harmful" hawk because it preyed on what they called "beneficial" songbirds. Now that ecologists have given us better under-

standing of the inner workings of wildlife communities we realize that songbirds, like all other living things, produce surpluses that can be harvested without affecting the year-to-year breeding stock. No species can be termed good or bad. Each has its place in one of the many food chains that bind all wildlife together in interdependent communities. Each community can support only so many individuals of a certain kind; the surplus serving as food for other species.

(Finally, an explanation of why zombies want to eat us!)

The classic style is not the only approach to writing that explains illustrations, photographs, informational graphics, slide shows, and other visual artifacts. One charming example is a photo book titled *Out on the Porch,* in which famous or picturesque southern front porches are displayed next to a literary text written for a different purpose but in the same spirit.

One photo, for example, is shot from behind two empty rockers on the front porch of Rowan Oak, William Faulkner's home near Oxford, Mississippi. Adjacent is a quotation from his novel *Absalom, Absalom!:*

It was a summer of wisteria. The twilight was full of it and of the smell of his father's cigar as they sat on the front gallery after supper until it would be time for Quentin to start, while in the deep shaggy lawn below the veranda the fireflies blew and drifted in soft random.

The texts from the bird guide were written to be informative and transparent in their authority, to be read through once and then acted upon. How different the quotation taken from Faulkner, which is dreamy and humid, a celebration of the senses, a text one can linger over with a cold drink on a warm evening.

These two forms—the classic and the literary—were often brought together in one of America's most important magazines: *Life*. From the 1930s into the 1960s and beyond, *Life* was America's photo magazine. Known more for its images than for its prose, *Life,* in fact, often recruited some of the world's best-known writers for projects, while some of its best writing was reserved for the captions of amazing photographic images.

I have a small collection of *Life* magazines from the World War II and Vietnam eras, and I found a typical example of its marriage of words and pictures in the June 27, 1969, edition. A five-page spread displays the work of the photographer Bob Gomel, who captures the early glory of the Rolls-Royce automobile in all its gilded and dreamy opulence. The name of the photographer is displayed prominently, of course, but it took a bit of a search to identify the caption writer, John Neary. Here is the paragraph that runs adjacent to the image of an astonishing gold-tinted Rolls:

> For its elegant quiet—even at top speed—this coffin-hooded behemoth was christened "The Silver Ghost" when it was built in 1907. Today, gilded by the twilight sun of Central Park and hardly showing its half-million miles, the car seems just that—the gleaming specter of an impossible long-ago era. The ancient Rolls-Royces shown on these pages were brought together by their

owners from both sides of the Atlantic for a recent tour of the Eastern U.S. In a time of assembly-line sameness they survive as bench marks of craftsmanship that wedded superb mechanical functions to an undeniable honesty of form. Perhaps no other cars inspire in their owners such pride or zealous devotion—the kind Hemingway had in mind when he wrote that a man has an obligation to a vehicle. Rolls-Royce fanciers find in the burnished patina of a mahogany steering wheel and the haughty sweep of a fender a sculptured beauty on wheels.

I love that 156-word paragraph for its enthusiasm, attention to detail, and diction, but also for its restraint. In the wrong hands, or for strictly marketing purposes, phrases like "bench marks of craftsmanship" or "burnished patina" or "haughty sweep of a fender" could feel overwrought and manipulative, like the "rich Corinthian leather" of Ricardo Montalban fame. But there's nothing for sale here, only a memory of past glory captured in words and pictures.

One of the world's great news designers, Mario Garcia, has on more than one occasion argued that the symbiotic pattern established over decades in *Life* magazine could and should be revitalized as a model for how words and pictures might work online. There is rich potential in this idea, but what Garcia suggests would not be easy. In some utopia, the same person who took brilliant photographs or videos could also write the texts that would help bring them to life. In the real world, such harmony is created by two, perhaps three, players: A great photographer. A collaborative writer. And an editor who can get the best from both of them.

GRACE NOTES

1. Look at some captioned illustrations or photos. Check the accuracy of the information in the text and the photo to make sure they do not contradict each other—unless the purpose of the caption is to correct the impression left by an image: "While it appears that high school student Roy Clark is using study hall to brush up on his algebra, behind that math textbook is the most recent issue of *Mad* magazine."

2. Some of the best advice on how to write to and with visual images comes from television writers and producers. In his book *Television News,* Ivor Yorke writes, "In most cases, to repeat exactly what is happening on the screen is to waste a great opportunity to tell the viewer something worthwhile. The writer's skill lies in being able to convey what is not clear from the pictures." In *Aim for the Heart,* my Poynter colleague Al Tompkins argues that in good television, "pictures and words should not match," but they should, according to Jill Geisler, "hold hands."

3. Examples of such hand-holding can be found in *American Moments,* a print version of the brief television features by Charles Kuralt. One black-and-white image from a firehouse shows an ancient lightbulb, its curly filament still aglow. Kuralt writes, "Think of it. Behind that handblown glass, those thick carbide filaments have been glowing for ninety-six years. From the time of Teddy Roosevelt, to our time. From horse-drawn hose carts to long yellow trucks. From a couple of years before Kitty Hawk to a generation after man's landing on the moon."

4. More tips:

- All the players—writer, editor, artist, designer— should understand the *focus* of the story.
- The elements of words and visuals should not compete for individual attention but work together in support of the focus.
- To test this collaboration, ask whether the combination of words and visual elements creates a singular *tone, style, mood,* or *effect.*

5. As an exercise, take a very short form such as the headline, subheadline, blurb, or caption and blow it up to a length where, with added details or insights, it accomplishes something more than expected.

31

~~~

Summarize and define.

Not all definitions are short, and not all appear in dictionaries. A well-traveled form of written composition is one in which the author tries to capture the meaning of concepts such as equality, death, religion, prostitution, identity, parenting, nature, marketing, time, war, gender, deviancy, and all the rest. In an influential essay titled "Defining Deviancy Down," former U.S. senator Daniel Patrick Moynihan explored ways in which behaviors once thought deviant (bearing a child out of wedlock) become tolerated, approaching normal. How you define deviancy matters greatly, argued Moynihan. If it is too easy to be marked as deviant, you probably live in an authoritarian country (consider the plight of women in places such as Saudi Arabia, where a woman's driving a car or not wearing a head covering would be considered deviant). On the other hand, if you live in a place where it is hard to be deviant (consider the extent to which pornography has moved to the mainstream of American culture), the lack of social norms can prove harmful, especially to the most vulnerable.

Building such brainy arguments requires months or years of study and thousands of words of scholarly prose. Or I could look up *deviant* in the *American Heritage Dictionary:* "Differing from a norm or from the accepted standards of a society." In no way could the dictionary definition match the power of Moynihan's argument. But it does have one advantage: it is short.

I am a freak who reads dictionaries for pleasure. My patron saint is a young man named Ammon Shea, who spent a year reading the *Oxford English Dictionary* from cover to cover, a journey described in *Reading the OED: One Man, One Year, 21,730 Pages.* Shea writes,

> I collect words.
>
> One could also say that I collect word books, since by last count I have about a thousand volumes of dictionaries, thesauri, and assorted glossaries, but I don't see that as a collection. These books are merely the tools with which I gather my collection. Although the books may be physical objects that take up room in my apartment, the real collection is the one that takes up all the room in my head, providing me with endless fascination and amusement as I move through the day, constantly thinking "There's a word for that...."

I testify to the idea that reading dictionaries provides "endless fascination and amusement." I am also struck by Shea's collection, a thousand volumes containing millions of words; and yet, by one definition, Shea's lexicons are anthologies of short pieces of writing—definitions, etymologies, usage notes, and glosses of words and phrases compiled in alphabetical order.

Shea's own book operates the same way. Having read every word and every definition and the almost two million historical citations in the *OED*, Shea curated this massive collection and offers readers the highlights, what ESPN might call "the plays of the day." After giving us the word, its part of speech, and a basic definition, Shea (a talented jazz musician) riffs on them for our fascination and amusement. Let's peruse Shea's book, pausing to enjoy strange words beginning with the letter *m:*

- "*Malesuete* (adj.) Accustomed to poor habits or customs. A nice, middle-of-the-road word for describing the common flaws that afflict us all. *Malesuete* does not refer to the catastrophic, hair-pulling, Greek tragedy kinds of flaws, such as being the kind of person who sacrifices his own children. It is more apt for describing things like clipping your toenails in public: the minor flaws that annoy everyone around you."
- "*Matrisate* (v.) To imitate a mother. Unlike most of the other words in the OED having to do with resembling or imitating a mother, *matrisate* is entirely judgment-free, allowing you to utilize it as you see fit, and without fear of reprisal."
- "*Micturient* (adj.) Having a strong desire to urinate. I rarely think this, but I am firmly of the opinion that the OED

dropped the ball—not with this word, which is admirably defined, but with its cousin: *cacaturient*. In the quote provided for *micturient* both words are used, yet *cacaturient* is not defined in the dictionary. Although it is easy enough to deduce its meaning in this context, I still think it was robbed."

Such is the fascination in the process of defining and then glossing the meaning and history of individual words. And while Shea doesn't believe a dictionary definition should be written to amuse, he applauds the way readers—none more than he—can find amusement in even a small act of lex.

A hero of lexicographers, Samuel Johnson towers over the eighteenth century like a lighthouse. In 1755, Johnson completed a decade of work in publishing *A Dictionary of the English Language*. In our time, this lexicon of more than forty thousand entries is best known for its few eccentric and politically charged definitions, such as those for *whig, tory*, and most famously *oats*: "A grain, which in England is generally given to horses, but in Scotland supports the people." (As I write this, in January 2011, a constitutional debate rages in Great Britain around the efforts of some Scots, probably still pissed at Dr. Johnson, to seek independence from England.)

In spite of such anomalies, most of the definitions in the dictionary are dead serious and straight shooting, according to Jack Lynch, who has edited a selection. He quotes Dr. Johnson on the tough intellectual work required for the task: "To interpret a language by itself is very difficult; many words cannot be explained by synonimes [synonyms] because the idea signified by them has not more than one appellation; nor by paraphrase, because simple ideas cannot be described.... To explain requires the use of terms less abstruse than that which is to be explained, and such terms cannot always be found."

Imagine being in Dr. Johnson's study the day he began to look through his historical citations for various meanings of the word *death*. The following definitions made it into his dictionary:

1. The extinction of life; the departure of the soul from the body....
2. Mortality; destruction....
3. The state of the dead....
4. The manner of dying....
5. The image of mortality represented by a skeleton....
6. Murder, the act of destroying life unlawfully....
7. Cause of death....
8. Destroyer....
9. [In poetry.] The instrument of death....
10. [In theology.] Damnation; eternal torments.

Definitions are not just for dictionaries or term papers, as we can see from modern biomedical and ethical debates about the definition of legal death. In 1976, an Oxford professor of law, P. D. G. Skegg, argued "for the enactment of a statute specifying when a person should be regarded as dead for legal purposes." What does it mean to be "brain dead" or in a "vegetative state"? Skegg wrote that "the key provision [of a law] could state simply that 'a person shall be regarded as dead for legal purposes when all brain activity (including brain stem activity) has irreversibly ceased.' This provision would leave the medical profession free to develop new and better criteria for determining when all brain activity had irreversibly ceased, and in this context committees of experts would undoubtedly have a part to play." In the past three decades—especially because of sensational cases such as those of Karen Ann Quinlan in New Jersey and Terri Schiavo in Florida—the definition of death has been argued in countless books and studies, using thousands if not millions of words. Yet when we get down to brass tacks, we desire brevity: "a person shall be regarded as dead for legal purposes when all brain activity (including brain stem activity) has irreversibly ceased." Professor Skegg's version contains only twenty-one words.

From the deadly serious, we turn to the delightfully twisted television comic and fake news talk show host Stephen Colbert, whose clueless persona has become an American icon. Through broad irony, Colbert builds his review of politics on sharp critiques of language, especially the narratives and arguments of presidential candidates and members of Congress. A special feature of his show is "The Word," and yes, I have an app for that on my iPhone.

The list of Colbert's political buzzwords and clichés includes such phrases as the follwing:

Bite the hand that feeds you
Bully pulpit
Catch 2012
Death and taxes
Economic boom
Happy endings
Head in the cloud

Hear no evil
Let them buy cake
Life, liberty and the pursuit of angriness
Over-reactor
Shock the vote
The 1%
The defining moment
Too big to nail

None of these words has had the impact of one of Colbert's earliest coinages: *truthiness*. It was introduced by Colbert on the October 17, 2005, episode of his show *The Colbert Report*. As he explained to his audience:

> We're not talking about *truth*, we're talking about something that seems like truth — the truth we want to exist.... Now I'm sure some of the "word police," the "wordinistas" over at *Webster's* are gonna say, "Hey, that's not a word." Well, anybody who knows me knows I'm no fan of dictionaries or reference books. They're elitist. Constantly telling us what is or isn't true. Or what did or didn't happen.

But can Colbert's neologism be captured in a dictionary definition? In 2006, *Merriam-Webster's* celebrated *truthiness* as its 2006 Word of the Year:

> truthiness (noun)
> 1 : "truth that comes from the gut, not books" (Stephen Colbert, Comedy Central's "The Colbert Report," October 2005)

2 : "the quality of preferring concepts or facts one wishes
     to be true, rather than concepts or facts known to be
     true" (American Dialect Society, January 2006)

That first definition is conveyed in eight words; the second,
in twenty-one.

GRACE NOTES

The craft of definition belongs to writers in all disciplines. At
its most basic, it involves a process of understanding, setting the limits of language, and conveying meaning. It meets
the standards of learning in the classroom, the study, and
the workplace. Just as I study the swings of professional
golfers to improve my play, so I study the work of professional definers to improve my writing. They are called
lexicographers.

For formal advice on how to write good definitions, I
was directed to the work of Sidney I. Landau, especially his
book *Dictionaries: The Art and Craft of Lexicography*. He
begins with the recognition that different writers are called,
by virtue of their mission and purpose, to define things in
different ways according to different standards. Even so, all
writers can learn from what Landau describes as "good
defining practice." To paraphrase his advice:

1. Give priority to the essence of a word or thing: "Definers must put themselves in the place of someone who hasn't
the vaguest idea what the word means and try to anticipate
the kinds of wrong assumptions such a person might make

about each draft of their definition, until they have written a definition that cannot be misunderstood."

2. Simplify, but not at the risk of clarity and comprehensibility. This has led to the practical wisdom that a definer should "avoid including difficult words in definitions of simpler words," which is a clear mandate that is often impossible to follow, as it was for Dr. Johnson, who defined *network* as "any thing reticulated or decussated, at equal distances, with interstices between the intersections." My rule of thumb: Use *charitable* to define or explain *eleemosynary*, but not the other way around.

3. Keep it short, but not so short that it creates ambiguity. Landau divides the labor of definition between the writer of the definition and the editor. This makes sense, even if the definer has no teacher or editor to lean on. The advice for the writer is to use as many words as are necessary to do the job, and then to cut. The goal is to make the definition accurate, clear, and comprehensible. Think of the effort the way you might approach writing a tweet. You may have an absolute 140-character limit to your message, but there is no reason not to begin with a 180-character draft. The handy (and dictatorial) Twitter counter shows you that you have run 40 characters too long. Let the cutting down to size begin!

4. Understand your audience. Beyond lexicography, the good writer is a good explainer. With knowledge of readers and their needs, the writer translates jargon, builds definitions based on what is already known, and leads an audience to greater clarity and new knowledge.

32

~~~

List.

One of America's great champions of clear writing was Robert Gunning, famous for his advice in *How to Take the Fog out of Writing*. In 1964, Gunning wrote:

> Suppose two letters come to your desk at the same time. One is a solid block of tightly spaced type. The other is generously broken into paragraphs, and includes indentation, enumeration, and possibly subheads. Which will you pick up first?
>
> We always choose the page that is lightened with white space. We do this because we know from long experience that a letter or report so written is better organized. The writer has tried to make the relationships between his ideas clearer. And every step he takes in this direction makes reading easier for us.

In his book *Write Tight*, William Brohaugh has a name for this strategy: nonverbal streamlining. "Writing tight involves more than leaving out words," he writes. "It also involves laying out words—laying them out on the page, the physical presentation of your writing." Among reliable strategies, Brohaugh lists sidebars, subheads, footnotes, paragraphing, and checklists.

There was a time when Facebook was encouraging its users to list "25 Random Things About Me" on the character, personality, and habits of the individual author. My response at the time was "25 Non-Random Things About Writing Short." I have slightly revised that list for the purposes of this book, and you will recognize in it—to help you review—some strategies I've already covered, but you will also notice some new language and a few new ideas.

1. Keep a journal in which you practice short writing.
2. Practice short writing on small surfaces: Post-it notes, index cards, the palm of your hand.
3. A list of twenty-five is *not* an example of short writing. It's long writing with twenty-five short parts— which is cool.
4. The short bits make a long list more readable, in part because they generate white space, which pleases the eye.
5. Obey Strunk and White: "Omit needless words." (As you've seen, I changed my mind on this one.)
6. Beware: the infinite space on the Internet encourages airy prose.
7. The shorter the passage, the greater the value of each word.

8. Every short passage should contain one gold coin, a reward for the reader.

9. Obey Donald Murray: "Brevity comes from selection and not compression."

10. Obey Chip Scanlan: "Focus, focus, focus."

11. Obey Sir Arthur Quiller-Couch: "Murder your darlings" — that is, have the courage to cut those literary effects that you most like but that do not contribute to the focus.

12. Imagine a short piece from the get-go. Think sonnet, not epic.

13. Cut the weaker elements: adverbs, passive constructions, strings of prepositional phrases, puffy Latinate words.

14. The more powerful the message, the shorter the sentence: "Jesus wept."

15. Don't "dump" short messages. Revise, polish, and proofread everything.

16. Try your hand at short literary forms: the haiku or the couplet.

17. Read, study, and collect great examples of short writing, from the diaries of Samuel Pepys to the tweets of your favorite peeps.

18. The best place for an important word in a short passage is at the *end*.

19. Begin the story as close to the end as possible.

20. Food for thought: study the prose in fortune cookies and on Valentine candy hearts.

21. Cut big, then small. Prune the dead branches *before* you shake out the dead leaves.

22. Obey Blaise Pascal: you may need more time, not less, to write something good and short.
23. Discuss this editorial: "They say only the good die young. The Spanish dictator Francisco Franco died last night at the age of eighty-three. Seems about right."
24. Write a mission statement for your short writing. Keep it short.
25. Treat all short forms—headlines, captions, blurbs, blog posts, tweets, text messages—as distinctive literary genres.

The list, even a long one, turns out to be a reliable and practical form of short writing. Any page or screen that carries a list will shrink the grayness of a text by expanding the white space. This helps the writer in making decisions about the number of items and their order. The reader then takes over, seeing the list at a glance, then deciding whether to move from top to bottom or to graze through.

GRACE NOTES

1. The most important effect of any list is to create white space on the page, making for a relaxed visual environment in which information can be scanned and understood.

2. The best lists give each element the potential to stand alone as an aphorism or tip.

3. Look for opportunities to repeat elements in lists or echo others, as when I ask the reader to "Obey…"

4. Though I have numbered this list to create points of reference for study or discussion, I've been content to mark other lists with bullets. Be versatile and purposeful in your decisions about the formatting of lists.

5. Buy a popular magazine such as *Cosmopolitan* or *Men's Health*. Notice on the cover how many lists are promised: advice, tips, secrets. Now scan the magazine to see the variety of formats in which they are delivered.

33

Report and narrate.

Time is the coauthor of good judgment. I've said it on many occasions, especially when reporters are tempted to be first with breaking news rather than right, the kind of haste that results in false reports, such as those of the premature deaths of Mark Twain, Bob Hope, Steve Jobs, and Joe Paterno. Yes, they all died eventually—as will we all—but let's agree that it makes sense to get things right *before* you write.

Accuracy is the soul of credibility over time. If you can learn to be accurate *and* fast—whatever your field of authorship—the practice of great short writing is a neural twitch away. One of my teachers on this topic is Josh Benton, a curious young journalist who took his experience as a newspaper writer to Harvard's Nieman Foundation, where he has become an influential chronicler of new forms of writing.

His most salient insight is that eyewitness testimony

delivered on the spot can generate the same kind of narrative energy readers might expect from a magazine story or even a book-length account, versions that might take months or years to develop. Real-time accounts take the form of live blogs or microblogs, including Twitter feeds. From Benton's point of view, live reports online shift the writer and reader "from a news peg to the moment." Observant writing serves as a form of critical reportage, rather than standard commentary or self-expression.

A young writer from the *Toronto Star*, Joanna Smith, was the first reporter to capture my attention with the vivid quality of her eyewitness microblogging from the streets of Haiti, devastated by earthquake. Here is a stream of her Twitter dispatches from the scene:

- "Crowd watched him exhale blood. Little girl in blue/ white Dorothy dress pushed her way into mob to see."
- "Fugitive from prison caught looting, taken from police, beaten, dragged thru street, died slowly and set on fire in pile of garbage."
- "Luckner Lewis asked to send msg 2 Cda: 'We're v glad 2 c u in #Haiti bc we need ur help. Biggest prblm is the smelling,' sez in2 recorder."
- "Pile of garbage, some of it burnt, reeking on corner of Cana-Pevert. 2 chickens pecking it for spare crumbs."
- "2 men carry little girl on cardboard stretcher, her arms around their necks, leg in newly set cast, yelping."
- "Man shouting into megaphone to clear road for garbage truck. Told it is on its way to mass burial site. Following, but not sure."

- "Too dangerous to set up distribution point in notorious Cite Soleil slum now, but assessing. Org gangs trying 2 profit, says UN."

These events happened years ago, but I still find Smith's dispatches riveting, an instant time machine that puts me on the scene and forces me—in the best sense—to pay attention. Returning to the theories of Josh Benton, these tweets raise our interest because of their eyewitness immediacy, a narrative energy that often dissipates with time and writing in traditional news forms.

In this sense, microblogging and long-form narrative storytelling (a form that requires lots of time) are allies against the snore-inducing, monochromatic delivery of conventional reporting. While the straight reporter asks, "Is it a story?" says Benton, the blogger wonders, "Is it interesting?" While the traditional report seems fixed in time, the blog offers "an ongoing series of dispatches." And just as narrative writers try to define characters in stories, so bloggers "can make characters out of sources—and out of reporters, too."

One of Benton's heroes is an English poet and journalist named James Fenton, an apologist for "reporting in its natural state"—that is, the timely perspective of witnesses on the ground. Reporting from Manila in 1986 on the fall of President Ferdinand Marcos, Fenton wrote:

We ran up the grand staircase and turned right into the ante-room. And there sat Marcos himself, with Imelda and family all around him, and three or four generals to the right. They had chosen the ante-room rather than the main hall, for there were only a few journalists and cameramen, and yesterday's great array of military men was nowhere to be seen. I looked very closely at Marcos and thought: it isn't him. It looked like ectoplasm. Like the Mighty Mekon. It was talking in a precise and legalistic way, which contrived to sound both lucid and utterly nonsensical. It had its left hand under the table, and I watched the hand for a while to see whether it was being deliberately concealed. But it wasn't.

The work of Fenton allows Josh Benton to connect new and old forms of short writing, from the kinds of wire service dispatches that reported dramatic bursts of news and information following the Kennedy assassination to the kinds of amateur dispatches posted all over the world on cell phones and other mobile devices during protest movements in 2011. More and more, news is broken not through official channels but through the collective experience of the crowd, as when a 5.9 earthquake surprised the state of Virginia and other locations on the East Coast. Here are just a few immediate dispatches reported on Twitter:

- "Preliminary Magnitude for Earthquake is 5.8 on doi. gov/rpwVxc 4 minutes ago." (@marindave)
- "My editor here is joking about having an earthquake drill later. Or may not be joking?" (@brianstelter)
- "I ALSO FELT THE EARTHQUAKE!!!!! I'M PART OF THIS MOMENT!!!" (@michaelkruse)

- "BREAKING: Obama WH announces contingency planning for Locusts, Frogs, Potomac running red." (@jeffjarvis)
- "Potential future-of-news angles: Will this be the earthquake that kills newspapers? Should the NYT put quake news outside its paywall?" (@jbenton)

Ernesto Priego summarized the effect of thousands of such postings with this message to Josh Benton from Europe: "It was incredible how reports from all over America came in at blinding speed....Almost felt it in London in real time!"

The seeds of such immediacy were sown in the nineteenth century when time and space disappeared through the energy of the telegraph, the technology that liberated communication from the bonds of geography and transportation. Almost two centuries later, we can be in the mind and heart of an activist such as Teju Cole, whose worldview bridges Brooklyn, New York, and Lagos, Nigeria:

- "Mohammed Sabo of Rigar Isamiya Darazo is now a widower. On their way to the farm, he hacked his wife to death with a hoe."
- "And right there in Nigeria, amidst all the goons and thieves and assholes, is a real transformational leader Governor Fashola of Lagos."
- "Meanwhile in Bauchi, Sani Hamidu, an amateur dabbler in the dark arts, cut his grandson Sagiru to pieces, but no money appeared."

- "Things need to change. This is no way to live. The Question is whether they should change revolutionarily (i.e. instantaneously)."
- "But against this: the already robust catalogue of senseless deaths and pointless suffering. The intimate violences of a traumatized nation."
- "Revolution. Such a pretty word. Such an attractive notion. Until someone drags your parents out into the street."

Fiction writers are getting into the act, too. Just as novels and short stories have often comprised the exchange of letters or telephone conversations, they can now be narrated in forms that resemble or mimic digital texts. The ingenious novelist Jennifer Egan wrote a short story, titled "Black Box," for the June 4, 2012, issue of the *New Yorker*. Each section — forty-seven in all — is a box framed in black, containing several tweet-like sentences. Here, for example, is section 3:

Posing as a beauty means not reading what you would like to read on a rocky shore in the South of France.

Sunlight on bare skin can be as nourishing as food.

Even a powerful man will be briefly self-conscious when he first disrobes to his bathing suit.

It is technically impossible for a man to look better in a Speedo than in swim trunks.

If you love someone with dark skin, white skin looks drained of something vital.

For the record, this narrative advances with sentences that are 22, 10, 17, 17, and 14 words. Eighty words in all.

GRACE NOTES

1. After more than two centuries, the basic reporting questions remain the same: *who, what, where, when, why,* and *how.* In short forms, the savvy reporter will avoid cramming the Five W's into a text, focusing instead on one or two.

2. Reports become stories through this conversion table: *who* = character; *what* = scene; *where* = setting; *when* = chronology; *why* = motive; and *how* = how it happened.

3. While we live in an increasingly mediated world, chained to our laptops and iPhones, vivid reporting in real time requires immersion in actual experience, seeing things with your own eyes—from a computer conference to a plane crash—and capturing those miniscenes in a crafted imitation of real life.

4. Unless you are receiving Twitter feeds in real time, you wind up reading a sequence of reports upside down, with the last element at the top of the list. Try covering an event via Twitter in, say, a dozen tweets. Capture these tweets in a word document and then reverse their order, placing them in their natural chronology. What is the difference in reading them in reverse or straight chronological order?

34

⚡⚡⚡

Title.

Not long ago, I might have written what is called a "label" headline on a story about young Hawaiians moving to Alaska to find work: "Surfing the Alaska Pipeline." That turns out to be a title for a story that doesn't yet exist, with a pun that mixes Hawaiian sea sports with an Alaskan form of oil distribution. Now I would wipe out on my effort to use that title because of something called SEO—search engine optimization. In a world dominated by Google and other search engines, the favored strategy for titles is to use straight, nonmetaphorical language that contains key words of news and information. Those key words are most likely to be picked up by search engines, raising the profile of your story toward the top of the Google page. So to give my story a better chance of being linked to and distributed by others, it would need a different title, something like "Young

Hawaiians Head to Alaska Looking for Jobs in the Oil Industry." Notice how I've hit the key words: *Hawaiians, Alaska, jobs, oil.*

SEO, I feared, was killing the craft of the clever headline, replacing creativity with algorithmic blandness.

Let me try a little experiment. I wanted to name my first book on writing for Little, Brown *The Name of the Dog* because getting the name of a dog and putting that name in a story lends the tale a kind of particularity that readers love. This was, indeed, my favorite writing tool. The publisher, Michael Pietsch, decided the title should be *Writing Tools.*

In my latest Google search of that phrase, my book turns up on the top three links and many times after that. When I search for "the name of the dog," I get nothing but websites about puppies.

Like so many other new technological imperatives, the hegemony of SEO is being challenged in 2012 because of the increasing importance of social networks as a way of finding news. Call it SNO, if you will—social network optimization. More and more people are alerted by what their friends and followers are reading and learning on Facebook and Twitter, a development that has led the media expert Jeff Sonderman to write, "Say goodbye to SEO." But wait. That was the lead to a story with this headline: "Social Media Replacing SEO as Google Makes Search Results Personal," which turns out to be an SEO title if I ever saw one.

I, for one, will not stand by and let a phrase as ugly as *search engine optimization* destroy the craft of great headline and title writing. Back in 1940, two editors understood that the creative energy and practical truth of a great headline can never be at odds. In their famous work *Headlines and Deadlines,* Robert E. Garst and Theodore Bernstein wrote:

> A headline writer who boasted that he was engaged in producing a literary art form promptly would be set down as an intellectual climber. Yet such a boast would not be without basis. For the headline is a form of expression having fully as many standards to be met and requirements to be filled as, say, the sonnet or the triolet, with the important additional one of visual form. The difference, of course, lies in the end-all—in one case it is beauty, in the other utility.

In the traditional print world, the headline is crucial. In the world of online reading and writing, the headline reigns supreme. Online readers are scanners, making quick decisions on what to read and when to leave one text for another. It is often a headline that seals the deal.

Word choice and word order remain the globe and scepter of headline clarity, immediacy, and authority. Let's take, for example, two competing headlines harvested by Vanessa Fox, the author of valuable books on search engines, marketing, and online audiences. More precisely, she knows what people tend to read online—and why.

The news in question was a November 15, 2011, event in which demonstrators against Wall Street were rousted by New York City police. The Associated Press headline read, "Latest Developments in the Occupy Protests," followed by the news summary, "Police cleared New York City's Zuccotti Park early Tuesday so that sanitation crews could clean the site Occupy Wall Street protesters have inhabited for two months."

At about the same time, Bloomberg News went with the headline "NYC Police Remove OWS Protesters," followed by "New York City police in riot gear swept into a Lower Manhattan park early today to remove Occupy Wall Street demonstrators who had been camping there for more than eight weeks to protest income inequality." An analysis by Vanessa Fox revealed that the Bloomberg version generated many more links, a result, in part, of the differences in the headlines.

By SEO standards, every word counts in the Bloomberg headline, while the AP head falls flat. That's *new-school* word accounting, but as I suggested to Fox after she had shared these examples with a group of writers, the Bloomberg headline is better written by *old-school* standards as well. There's no verb in the AP headline! No verb means no action. No action means nothing for the reader to see. Nothing to see means no fire in the brain and no reason to dive deeper into the story. Bloomberg by contrast begins with subject and verb and ends with the direct object: police remove protesters. It captures a scene with purpose, played out with vigor in the summary, which adds "riot gear," "camping," "eight weeks" (more dramatic than two months), and "to protest income inequality" as a kicker.

The moral here is simple: No newfangled formula can replace the one-two-three power of essential reporting and storytelling. In the end, someone does something to somebody, and we want to know more about it, a form of reader interest optimization that we still call SVO: subject, verb, object.

GRACE NOTES

1. Spend time and energy on titles and headlines. They matter for the book, the blog post, and more. The original subtitle for *How to Write Short* was something like "Effective Communication in an Accelerating Age," but no one liked all those long words in a book that honored the short. The revision: "Word Craft for Fast Times." In a title or headline, every word, every letter, every space, counts.

2. Pay attention to the effect of your headline or title language on search engines. But realize the extent to which the Google search is being challenged by the expanding influence of social networks. While SEO requires a literal account of content, social networks tolerate more creative and casual language, with Twitter spreading its messages via hashtags, organizing index marks introduced by #, such as #writingtools, #myfirsttime, #OccupyWallStreet, #Haitiquake, and #Romneysdog. The humble hashtag, argues the social media expert Sree Sreenivasan, can direct readers' attention in a powerful way if it appears as "the shortest possible unique and memorable phrase." That's not a bad description of all good short writing.

3. The secret formula for a good online headline: a sentence that contains the two or three essential elements of news and information constructed in SVO form (subject, verb, object): "President Obama Lends Support to Gay Marriage." Do not be afraid to add something distinctive—a grace note—that sets your work apart, as in this plagiarism case: "Ethics Professor Commits Unoriginal Sin." When you see such effective titles, copy them in your daybook.

35

~~~

Protect against the misuses
of short writing.

We've talked over and over again about the disproportionate power of short writing without focusing enough attention on the power to harm. Let's return, for example, to the slogan as a familiar and persuasive piece of writing. There is a problem with the slogan, of course, getting back to our historical notion that it derives from a Scots war chant. The slogan— related in some ways to the contemporary "sound bite" or "talking point"—has been central to the work of propaganda and misinformation, an appeal to emotions such as fear and prejudice rather than to reason and tolerance.

Attachment to a slogan can also become a substitute for healthy skepticism and critical thinking, a problem Jeffrey Scheuer attacks in his book *The Sound Bite Society:* "A sound bite society is one that is flooded with images and slogans,

bits of information and abbreviated or symbolic messages—a culture of instant but shallow communication. It
is not just a culture of gratification and consumption, but
one of immediacy and superficiality, in which the very
notion of 'news' erodes in a tide of formulaic mass entertainment. It is a society anesthetized to violence, one that is cyn-
ical but uncritical, and indifferent to, if not contemptuous
of, the more complex human tasks of cooperation, concep-
tualization, and serious discourse."

Two great British writers, both known for their dystopian
novels, have shaped my own opinions on issues of politics
and language. The first is George Orwell, who offered this
critique in the aftermath of World War II:

> In our time, political speech and writing are largely the
> defense of the indefensible. Things like the continuance
> of British rule in India, the Russian purges and deporta-
> tions, the dropping of the atom bombs on Japan, can
> indeed be defended, but only by arguments which are too
> brutal for most people to face, and which do not square
> with the professed aims of political parties. Thus political
> language has to consist largely of euphemism, question-
> begging and sheer cloudy vagueness.

He offers examples, such as when "defenseless villages are
bombarded from the air, the inhabitants driven out into the
countryside, the cattle machine-gunned, the huts set on fire
with incendiary bullets: this is called *pacification*." No need
to look for examples beyond our own time, when we argue
over whether waterboarding is torture or a form of

"enhanced interrogation." Are those who sneak across the border from Mexico to the United States "illegal aliens" or "undocumented workers"? In our time, controversial issues come down to a war of words, to a struggle to see who can gain the high ground of language. Don't think such language is arrived at through trial and error. It is arrived at by researchers and through focus groups, whose responses to messages are measured by partisans and spin doctors.

In his book *Words That Work*, the so-called public opinion guru Frank Luntz argues that "it's not what you say, it's what people hear." As a language researcher who often appears on Fox News, Luntz offers advice on the language that moves an argument or an issue forward. In short, propaganda.

"So if you are an advocate of 'less' government," writes Luntz, "better to use the language of *making Washington accountable* or *making Washington more effective*." Here are a few of the word choices promoted by the opinion guru:

- When speaking of health care reform, never say *privatization;* say *personalization.*
- Never say *tax reform* or *tax cuts;* instead say *tax simplification* or *tax relief.*
- Never say *capitalism* or *global economy;* say *free market economy.*
- Never say *inheritance tax* or *estate tax;* say *death tax.*
- Never say *drilling for oil;* say *exploring for energy.*

If you believe in what is sometimes called tort reform, Luntz suggests that you refer to opponents not as *trial lawyers,* but as *personal injury lawyers.* Why? "It is difficult to distrust a *trial lawyer,* in part because we see them portrayed so favorably on television and in the movies. But *personal injury lawyers,* also known as *ambulance chasers,* remind people of those annoying, harassing, middle-of-the-night TV commercials cajoling us to sue someone. If you want to get an additional level of intensity, talk about *predatory personal injury lawyers.*"

There is no neutrality here, no need for objectivity or nonpartisanship. Part of the art of selling is to get you to choose Pepsi over Coke, Ford over Chevy, Republican over Democrat. Instead of language neutrality, the spin doctors require language loading. A case in point would be the preference for *exploring for energy* over *drilling for oil.* Notice how Luntz moves the message up the ladder of abstraction from the visual, visceral imagery of huge drill bits penetrating the earth, resulting in geysers of black goo, to language that is hard to visualize. The move is described in this Orwell critique: "The inflated style is itself a kind of euphemism. A mass of Latin words falls upon the facts like soft snow, blurring the outlines and covering up all the details. The great enemy of clear language is insincerity. When there is a gap between one's real and one's declared aims, one turns as it were instinctively to long words and exhausted idioms, like a cuttlefish squirting out ink."

So what are we to make of historical slogans that remain memorable over generations: "Remember the Alamo," or "Remember the *Maine,*" or "Loose lips sink ships," or "Fifty-four forty or fight!" (a slogan I love for its numbered alliteration, even though I can't remember what the issue was about)? (From Dictionary.com: "a slogan popular in 1846, especially among Democrats, who asserted U.S. ownership of the entire Oregon country, including the part that Great Britain claimed between 49° and 54° 40'; N latitude.")

In 1958 that other great dystopian, Aldous Huxley, argued that dictatorship by violence and suppression—as dramatized in Orwell's *1984*—may be replaced by "reinforcements and manipulations," described in his own novel *Brave New World*. To arrive at that conclusion, Huxley draws a distinction between rational and nonrational forms of propaganda.

He writes, "Propaganda in favor of action that is consonant with enlightened self-interest appeals to reason by means of logical arguments based upon the best available evidence fully and honestly set forth." The triumph of reason over passion would create a utopia. Instead, writes Huxley, "Propaganda in favor of action dictated by the impulses that are below self-interest offers false, garbled or incomplete evidence, avoids logical argument and seeks to influence its victims *by the mere repetition of catchwords,* by the furious denunciation of foreign or domestic scapegoats, and by cunningly associating the lowest passions with the highest ideals, so that atrocities come to be perpetrated in the name of God." (The italics are mine.)

These arguments lead to an inescapable conclusion: that short writing, however crafty and clever, can be used (and has been used countless times) for evil purposes as well as good. There are many good things to sell in this world, from useful products to progressive ideas. Your soul isn't one of them.

GRACE NOTES

1. In your reading and your crafting of short writing, be alert to the potential abuses of the form. Keep a special place in your daybook for the most egregious examples, which can be found daily on radio talk shows or in cable news commentary, or cyclically in political ads. Note the example: "will not refer to immigrants or workers, only to illegal aliens." You might then underline the abuse: "seeks to dehumanize with the word *aliens,* which sounds as if the United States is being attacked by Martians."

2. The word *propaganda* once had a neutral meaning: language or other messages in support of a candidate or cause. By the end of World War II, it took on negative connotations, with associations to Nazi hate speech and literature. As a result, we no longer have a word that stands for positive, rational propaganda. Perhaps *advocacy* comes close. Keep your eyes open for language—including slogans and other ways of summarizing—that encourages reason over emotions and passions.

A Few Final Words —
441 to Be Exact

Congratulations. If you have come this far, you have read more than fifty thousand words on the topic of short writing. I hope you think I have proven my case: that in the hands of careful writers, a few good words can be worth a thousand pictures.

I have tried to make transparent my philosophy of writing: that achievement in craft only matters when attached to a noble purpose, or at least a useful one. I learned this notion from a friend killed in a car crash not long ago. He was Cole Campbell, a controversial newspaper editor who became an important academic leader and essayist. In a recent collection of his work, *Journalism as a Democratic Art,* I discovered the source of Cole's reflections on writing with a purpose. It was a 1999 book, *For Common Things,* written by "a wise young West Virginian" named Jedediah Purdy. (I know that Cole just loved the author's name.)

Purdy wrote,

> A marriage of commitment and knowledge produces dignified work.
>
> I think of this achievement through the idea of the craftsman, perhaps because I have known craftsmen well and admired their work, perhaps because the solidity of their labor ties ideas to sound and reliable things. His enduring quality of dignity arises from the fact that his work is luminous to him, in its process and its purpose. He understands the application of every tool he uses; many of them he may be able to make or repair himself. He can judge the quality of his materials because he understands what they must contribute to his product and just how that contribution will be made. Because he understands the use of his product as well, he knows just what it is to make it well or badly.

For Cole, it was those three elements—purpose, craft, and use—that made work "luminous" and life worth living.

Purdy's description of craftsmen—without specificity—suggests the work of carpenters, potters, or boatwrights. But the integrity he describes applies as well to the work of writers' hands. W. H. Auden, remember, said that a poem was a "contraption"—a made thing—with someone hiding inside it. In literature, the poem does it best, of course: it generates a power in language out of proportion to the length of the work. In the end, short work need not be a compromise forced on the writer by technology, evolving social habits, or shrinking resources. The great writer, working in the short form, can look back on the history of writing for sources of inspiration and can build on the tradition of word craft—even in these fast times.

PERMISSIONS AND CREDITS

〜〜〜

How to Write Short contains hundreds of examples of short writing, ranging in length from a single word to three hundred words. Each example is used for an educational purpose, to illustrate a strategy of the writing craft.

Finding and verifying these examples—some ancient, others brand-new—proved quite a challenge. Some citations turned out to be apocryphal. Others were misattributed. Others, having been transformed through revision and transcription, survive in multiple forms.

Under the guidance of my editors at Little, Brown, I've done my best to verify each example and give appropriate credit to the author and/or the published source. In the age of instant messages, blogs, Twitter, and Facebook, standards of authorship, fair use, and common courtesy should still apply, even as they are adapted to innovative technologies and new forms of expression. With that in mind, we thank the following authors and publishers for their permission to reprint examples of short writing, and, beyond that, offer credit to many authors whose work influenced mine:

"Insomnia" reprinted with permission of Val Gryphin; "Peanut Butter" reprinted with permission of Camille Esses, "Visiting Hours" reprinted with permission of Katrina Robinson, all published in *Hint Fiction,* edited by Robert Swartwood, W. W. Norton, 2010.

Tweets by David B. Thompson, Michael T. Rose, Stephanie Hayes, and Jay Rosen reprinted with permission. Excerpts from *The World According to Twitter* reprinted with permission of David Pogue and Black Dog Publishing.

Excerpts from *Not Quite What I Was Planning* and *Smith Magazine's* Six-Word Memoir project (www.smithmag.net/sixwords) reprinted with permission of Larry Smith.

Work previously appearing on the Poynter Institute website (www.poynter.org) is reprinted with permission of its editor, Julie Moos.

Excerpts from workshops by CBS Radio News correspondent Peter King reprinted with his permission.

"Beer Can" from *Assorted Prose* by John Updike, copyright © 1965, copyright renewed 1993 by John Updike (originally published in *The New Yorker*). Reprinted by permission of Alfred A. Knopf, a division of Random House, Inc.

While doing research for *How to Write Short*, I gathered a small library of books, articles, and artifacts that shed light on the craft. I have decided not to try to track down and identify the authors of texts on old baseball cards, fortune cookies, and cereal boxes, but they get special recognition here. They taught me how to read.

Special credit and thanks go to the following authors, editors, and publishers as excellent sources of knowledge about effective short writing. Citations for books come from the editions on my shelves, not necessarily the most recent:

Tom Petty and Jeff Lynne, for the lyrics of "Free Fallin'," sheet music published by the Hal Leonard Corporation.

Nick Douglas, editor, *Twitter Wit*, Harper Collins, 2009. (One of the first books to identify Twitter as a source of good writing.)

Garry Wills, *Lincoln at Gettysburg*, Simon & Schuster, 1992. (How Lincoln revolutionized political language.)

Wieden+Kennedy, the Oregon agency that created the Chrysler ad "Halftime in America."

Eva Talmadge and Justin Taylor, *The Word Made Flesh*, Harper Perennial, 2010. (Collection of literary tattoos.)

Isaac Metzker, editor, *A Bintel Brief*, Schocken, 1971. (Powerful advice for new Jewish immigrants.)

Blanche Ebbutt, *Don't for Husbands, Don't for Wives*, reprint, A. & C. Black, Ltd., 1913.

Meyer Berger, *Meyer Berger's New York*, Random House, 1960. (One of the *New York Times*'s greatest writers.)

Tom Parker, *Rules of Thumb*, Houghton Mifflin, 1983.

Charles Kuralt, *Charles Kuralt's American Moments*, Simon & Schuster, 1998.

Yahia Lababidi, *Signposts to Elsewhere*, Jane Street Press, 2008.

George Plimpton, editor, *The Writer's Chapbook*, Modern Library, 1999. (From the *Paris Review* interviews.)

Dorothy Carnegie, editor, *Dale Carnegie's Scrapbook*, Simon & Schuster, 1959.

Joshua Kendall, *The Man Who Made Lists*, Putnam, 2008. (How Roget got started.)

Windsor Mann, editor, *The Quotable Hitchens*, Da Capo, 2011.

W. H. Auden and Louis Kronenberger, *The Viking Book of Aphorisms*, Barnes & Noble, 1966.

Ammon Shea, *Reading the OED*, Perigee, 2008. (Adventures in lexicography.)

Christopher Johnson, *Microstyle*, Norton, 2011. (The first good book about short writing.)

Joseph M. Williams, *Style*, Longman, 2003.

James Geary, *The World in a Phrase*, Bloomsbury, 2005.

Dag Hammarskjöld, *Markings*, Ballantine, 1983.

Richard H. Pough, *Audubon Guides*, Doubleday, 1951.

Lou Beach, *420 Characters*, Houghton Mifflin Harcourt, 2011. (Stories in the form of Facebook status updates.)

Gene Weingarten, *Old Dogs: Are the Best Dogs*, Simon & Schuster, 2008.

Robert Byrne, editor, *The 2,548 Best Things Anybody Ever Said*, Simon & Schuster, 2006.

William Brohaugh, *Write Tight*, Writer's Digest, 1993.

Robert Garst and Theodore Bernstein, *Headlines and Deadlines*, Columbia, 1940.

Jey Heinrichs, "A Story's Secret Ingredient," in *Spirit*, October 2011, p. 82.

Dorothy Parker, *The Best of Dorothy Parker*, Duckworth, 1984.

Cor van den Heuvel, editor, *The Haiku Anthology*, Fireside, 1986.

José Saramago, *The Notebook*, Verso, 2010.

William Strunk Jr. and E. B. White, *The Elements of Style*, Macmillan, 1959.

Sidney I. Landau, *Dictionaries*, Cambridge, 2001.

Jack Lynch, editor, *Samuel Johnson's Dictionary*, Levenger, 2002.

Alvin Redman, editor, *The Epigrams of Oscar Wilde*, Bracken, 1995.

The Collected Poems of Emily Dickinson, Barnes & Noble, 1993.

Laurence Urdang and Celia Dame Robbins, *Slogans*, Gale, 1984.

Reynolds Price, editor, *Out on the Porch*, Algonquin, 1992.

Arthur H. Bell, *How to Write Attention-Getting Memos, Letter, and E-mails*, Barron's, 2004.

Michael Schmidt, editor, *The Great Modern Poets*, Quercus (2006).

Joseph Sugarman. *The Adweek Copywriting Handbook*, Wiley, 2007.

Frank Luntz, *Words That Work,* Hyperion, 2007.

Ben Schott, *Schott's Original Miscellany,* Bloomsbury, 2002.

Rosemary Ahern, *The Art of the Epigraph,* Atria, 2012.

Gloria Cooper, editor, "Correct Me If I'm Wrong," *Columbia Journalism Review* and the Newseum, 2008.

Ben Yagoda, *When You Catch an Adjective, Kill It,* Broadway, 2007.

Constance Hale and Jessie Scanlon, *Wired Style,* Broadway, 1999.

Chris Barr and the Senior Editors of Yahoo!, *The Yahoo! Style Guide,* St. Martin's Griffin, 2010.

Thanks to Eugene Patterson, editor, *Chord: The Old Testament Condensed,* self-published, 2012. I pay special homage to this work, edited by my dear friend Gene Patterson, who tackled the King James Bible at the age of eighty-nine while under hospice care. Gene's version cuts a half-million words from the original. The result, as the title indicates, is "The main chord, not the whole hymn."

Thanks to my college friend Joe Morrissey and his entire family for asking me to join in the process of choosing an epitaph for his brother, the folksinger and songwriter Bill Morrissey. His *Essential Collection* is available on Rounder Records.

Thanks to authors John Capouya and Frank Deford, to Scott Simon of NPR and Joanna Smith of the *Toronto Star,* to marketing expert Vanessa Fox for work that launched me toward a new understanding of short writing.

An inexhaustible supply of short writing—good and

bad—is available on the Internet. The following websites proved particularly helpful:

NYTimes.com
WashPost.com
CNN.com
TampaBay.com
Poynter.org
2Spare.com
Oddee.com
Match.com
Cupid.com
iVillage.com
MidlifeBachelor.com
MailOnline.uk
Dictionary.com

ACKNOWLEDGMENTS

This book is dedicated to Gene Patterson, one of America's great newspaper editors. Since 1977, Gene, who hired me to coach writers at the *St. Petersburg Times,* has served as friend and mentor. Before that, he had a legendary career at the *Atlanta Constitution.* From 1960 to 1968 he wrote a signed column—every day—for the editorial page, often about the issues of racial injustice. He had qualities that endeared him to that other great opinion shaper Ralph McGill, who saw in Patterson a special combination of physical and moral courage and the ability to "write like an angel."

Thanks to Jane Dystel, my agent, for steering a clear path for a writer who on occasion loses his way. Thanks to Michael Pietsch for supporting this project at Little, Brown, and for assembling an editorial, artistic, and marketing staff second to none. This is my fourth book since 2006 with editor Tracy Behar, who has become not just a literary guide, but a dear friend. To Keith Hayes, who once again hit the target with his cover design. To all the copy editors at LB who have held the net while I walked across the wire, especially to Rachel Careau, Karen Wise, and Betsy Uhrig.

The year 2012 marks thirty-five years since my arrival in St. Petersburg, Florida. I owe my development as both a writer and a teacher to the dedicated people who work at the *Tampa Bay Times* (formerly the *St. Petersburg Times*) and the Poynter Institute, a now world-renowned school for journalism and democracy.

Special thanks go to friends and family, most of whom think I would do well to follow my own advice about short writing. To Tom French, my writing buddy. To Juniper French, who makes me laugh, and her mom, Kelley Benham French. To Jeff Saffan, who fixes everything. To Mike Hartigan, who listens on the golf course. To my mother, Shirley Clark, who at ninety-three is still proud of me. To my dog Rex, who at nineteen is still proud of me. To my daughters, Alison, Emily, and Lauren, for their loyalty and love. Finally, to Karen, my wife of forty-one years. The shortest sentence I ever uttered in this world turned out to be the best: "I do."

INDEX

INDEX

INDEX

INDEX

ABOUT THE AUTHOR

〜〜〜

By some accounts, Roy Peter Clark is America's writing coach, a teacher devoted to creating a nation of writers. A PhD in medieval literature, he is widely considered the most influential writing teacher in the rough-and-tumble world of newspaper journalism. With a deep background in traditional media, Clark has illuminated the discussion of writing on the Internet. More than two million of his podcasts on the craft have been downloaded. He has gained fame by teaching writing to children and has nurtured Pulitzer Prize–winning authors such as Thomas French and Diana Sugg. He is a teacher who writes and a writer who teaches.

For more than three decades, Clark has taught writing at the Poynter Institute, a school for journalists in St. Petersburg, Florida, considered among the most prominent such teaching institutions in the world. He graduated from Providence College in Rhode Island with a degree in English and earned a PhD from Stony Brook University.

In 1977 he was hired by the *St. Petersburg Times* to become one of America's first writing coaches and worked with the American Society of Newspaper Editors to improve newspaper writing nationwide. Because of his work with ASNE, Clark was elected as a distinguished service member, a rare honor for a journalist who has never edited a newspaper. He was inducted into the Features Hall of Fame, an honor he shares with the likes of Ann Landers. He has served as Starr Writer-in-Residence at Vassar College, an honor he shares with authors such as Billy Collins, Tim O'Brien, and Salman Rushdie.

Clark has authored or edited seventeen books about writing and journalism, including his most recent, *Help! For Writers*, for which there is a mobile app.